C000244515

MY HORSE
REARS

Curing problem behaviour in horses
with kindness and consideration

Ruth Mazet

Event to Event

Photography & Video Production

www.eventtoevent.co.uk

phone: 07860 336429

email: evelyn@eventtoevent.co.uk

J.A. Allen
London

First published in Great Britain in 2012

J.A. Allen
Clerkenwell House
Clerkenwell Green
London EC1R 0HT

J.A. Allen is an imprint of Robert Hale Limited

www.allenbooks.co.uk

ISBN 978 0 85131 990 2

British Library Cataloguing in Publication Data
A catalogue record for this book is available from the British Library

Design by The Urban Ant Ltd

Printed in China by New Era Printing Company Ltd

Disclaimer of Liability
The author and publisher shall have neither liability nor responsibility to
any person or entity with respect to any loss or damage caused or alleged to
be caused directly or indirectly by the information contained in this book.
While the book is as accurate as the author can make it, there may be errors,
omissions, and inaccuracies. It is recommended that, whenever riding and
whilst dealing with behavioural problems in horses, a hard hat approved to
current safety standards be worn.

CONTENTS

PART 3 HANDLING ON THE GROUND

PREFACE

This book has been written primarily for what I call the 'pleasure rider'. Maybe this describes you. You have no ambition to become a top competition rider but just want to enjoy owning and riding your horse. You have found the horse of your dreams but, before too long, he starts getting difficult one way or another, even if only mildly so. And you can't understand why. The purpose of my book is to shine a light on the murky world of problem behaviour in horses. So much is said and written; so little is understood.

I have been working almost uniquely with problem horses for about thirty-five years and enjoyed every minute of it. Finding my way into the horse's heart and mind and gaining his complete trust and confidence is the challenge. Knowing that, at the end of it, this horse will now do whatever I want without any fuss or argument is the reward.

The cornerstone of my approach is to work with the horse's innate desire to please. Every horse has it – although sometimes it's deeply buried. The desire to please is an integral part of every horse's basic nature. It's designed to give them an easy life. When all is harmonious and life is easy for them, it's easy for us too!

Until now, no one has come up with what might be called 'a universal method' for curing problem behaviour that is consistently successful and can be used by anyone from the beginner to the more experienced. What is needed to resolve problems with horses is an understanding of the way the horse's mind works combined with a few relatively simple techniques – and here it all is; everything you need to know about solving problems with horses. As a methodology, it's foolproof. Anyone can do it. And I'm going to show you how.

ACKNOWLEDGEMENTS

The writing of this book was one thing which required only me and my computer, but putting it all together with all the photographs was something else entirely. My thanks must go to my daughter, Jess, for her endless patience and cooperation and the use of her very obliging horse, Ellie as a model of both good and bad behaviour.

Equally, I must thank Evelyn Radnai for her astonishing ability with a camera. I only had to tell her what I wanted and she got it for me. Thanks must also go to Lime Kiln Farm Equestrian Centre and staff for the use of their facilities and horses, and to Charmaine Atkins for the use of her facilities, also to Jean Le Fleming for the very kind use of her beautiful horse, Blaze. Thanks too, to Pete Ormosi for the loan of his posh camera.

Last, but not least, I must also thank my friend Andrea Rooney for her unwavering support and hours of listening to me rabbiting on about photo-shoots and the weather!

Illustration credits
Photos by, or provided by, the author, except for those on pages 34, 59, 75, 157 (top) by Bob Langrish and those on the following pages by Evelyn Radnai: 12, 19, 20–22, 26, 28, 43, 44, 46, 49–52, 64, 65, 68, 69, 71, 77, 82, 86, 92, 93, 95, 97, 98–101, 104, 107, 108, 109, 112, 114, 115, 117, 119, 120, 125, 126, 128, 129, 131 (lower), 132–135, 137–140, 143–148, 151–154, 163

Line illustrations by Dianne Breeze

INTRODUCTION

I have spent most of my adult life working almost exclusively with problem horses, but my career with horses did not start out that way. As a teenager, I had the good fortune to own and train my first horse; a 15.1hh old-style Welsh Cob x Thoroughbred called Babe. I had no previous experience, books or instructors to guide me. My training was done by instinct. I felt my way forward, mostly by asking the question 'I wonder what would happen if…'

'I wonder what would happen if I got on her back and sat on her'; 'I wonder what would happen if I asked her to carry me home' … stuff like that. I did have a rudimentary knowledge of riding. I had been to a riding school for a year, and then spent another couple of very happy years, pootling round the countryside on a borrowed pony called Ned. This pony never put a foot wrong – so I knew what I was aiming for. I wanted my horse to be just like Ned.

I succeeded – admirably. Anyone could ride my mare and several did. I lent her out freely to anyone who wanted to ride her. Not one of them ever said they had any problem whatsoever. I took that as normal. I had never had any problems with any horse I had ridden to date. Why should my horse be any different?

Babe became my standard. It seemed to me that all horses to be used for pleasure activities (including local-level competing) should be this way. Anything else was unacceptable. For people who just want to get on a horse and have a good ride, this is how a horse should be.

My next horse was a family cob, bought some years later as a three-year-old and also unbroken. Naturally, I had every confidence that I would train this cob to be as good as Babe. She was everything I expected. This time, when other people took her out for a ride, they would comment on how obedient and well-behaved she was. This surprised me. I took it as normal. Would I lend out a horse who was any other way?

However, Moony came with a problem I wasn't expecting. She was terrified of lorries and tractors. I couldn't understand why. Neither did I know what to do about it. Worse still, we trained her for driving, as that was what my husband wanted to do. A driving horse with a profound fear of lorries and tractors is a complete nightmare.

I regret to say that I made a right pig's ear of it in the beginning. The only 'treatment' I knew for a horse who wouldn't go was to use a whip. I didn't like doing it, but knew no other way. It didn't work. If anything, she got worse.

This bugged me. Of course, I wanted her to get better. Slowly, it dawned on me that there might be a better, gentler, easier way. I wonder what would happen if ... The only way to find out was to try it. I did – and it worked!

The next experience was a two-year-old, a 12.2hh pony called Swift. I bought him to break, train and sell on but he turned out to be such a cracking little pony that I kept him for my daughter. My unique and self-taught training method worked like a charm. Never before or since have I found a horse or pony who was so easy. He was so good that by the time he was four, I was giving riding lessons on him to complete beginners. At the time, this seemed very premature. According to the wisdom of the day, a riding horse was never considered to be fully mature (and therefore reliable) until he was about seven.

Swift never put a foot wrong, until my beginners started cantering off the lunge and out on a hack. He was fine on the lunge but, out in the open, going into canter, he promptly bucked them off. I couldn't understand that. He had never bucked in his life. Neither did I know what to do about it.

My life changed and I moved abruptly. My daughter started riding Swift. She was quite a good little rider and it didn't occur to me that Swift, now a seven-year-old, might buck. In any case, wasn't he now old enough to know better? But he did, as before – going into canter. Now, I really had to do something about it. This was my daughter's pony. The plan was that she would ride him for a good few years and bucking was not part of the plan. Naturally, I wanted her to have a safe, sensible pony – which, in every other respect, he was.

In the short term, the problem was solved. They went on to have a lot of fun doing everything you can do with a pony, including dressing up! But Jess told me many years later that Swift did still buck, but she had learned, not only how to sit it out and stay on, but – would you believe it, enjoy it and set poor little Swift up to do it some more. Thus she learned how to make a horse buck.

All this, I can tell you, was food for thought. I started asking more questions. Why did these things happen? What was the reason? What was the provocation, if any?

From this point on, I met nothing but problem horses and ponies. With every one of them, I learned some more. And with every one of them I found the way to overcome their problems and bring them back to what I call a 'normal' horse – one who is kind, gentle and friendly and above all, problem-free.

In 1989, I launched myself professionally as a peripatetic problem solver.

I knew how unsettling it was for a horse to move to a new home and that coming to me for training would only add to his problems. I also knew that the owner or rider had to know what to do. Otherwise, the problem was likely to start all over again. Reforming the horse in his own home was the obvious solution. That said, I did also occasionally have a horse sent to me when the problems were so numerous and/or severe that working with him on a daily basis was the only hope of a good outcome.

The turn of the century had an unexpected impact. I began to understand the full significance of the internet. A website could reach thousands, if not millions of people – and it stretched all over the world. My 'Help for Horse-riders' website www.horse-talk.org was born. I now counsel people with problem horses from all over the world.

It has been a long journey of discovery. Even now, I am sometimes presented with a horse problem I haven't met before – though not often, I hasten to add. It has to be said that after so many years' experience, it doesn't take long to work out the answer. There is logic to horse behaviour. Understand the way the logic works and it's not hard to work out the solution.

May I add that, once a horse has had a problem, the memory of it is always there. Given the trigger stimulus, he may revert to his previous behaviour – but that's OK. When we know what to do, it's not a problem any more, just a minor inconvenience.

This book aims to explain everything you need to know about how to deal with a problem horse and what to do about specific behaviours. At the same time, I have given you some background information to add to your general knowledge and understanding.

I hope you find this book interesting, informative, but above all – *useful*. It saddens me immensely that so many people have so many problems with their horses. There really is no need for it. But that's another story!

PART 1
BEFORE WE START
WORK ON THE HORSE…

Horses do not 'misbehave' without a good reason. I use the term 'misbehave' guardedly. *From the horse's point of view*, he is not misbehaving. Neither is he simply being naughty (horses don't know the meaning of the word!) He is merely doing what instinct tells him to do in any given situation. Everything the horse does is telling us something in 'horse-language'. He has no other. Horse language is one of body language and behaviour. It is also the window into his mind. We have to look through that window and see what's going on in there. What is he telling us?

When we know what he is saying, we can establish a dialogue. It goes something like this. He says, 'I don't like doing this.' We say, 'OK, we'll do something else!' This is extremely simplistic, but it gives the general idea. Before anything can be achieved, we must have communication.

Working with any horse, for whatever reason, requires, above all, a working knowledge of what makes the horse tick. What makes him do what he does? The horse is not a machine. Unlike a car, or a washing machine, we can't just turn the key or push a few buttons. We have to know how to get his willing cooperation.

We must also be sensitive to his needs and nature. We must know what he likes and dislikes. The horse has various characteristics that define him as a horse. Some of them are quite surprising. For example, doing anything energetic goes against horses' basic nature; it is not natural for them to expend energy unnecessarily. Neither do horses like being shut away in a box all night, although some who have been cosseted in the early years do like to get out of foul weather. Their apparent pleasure at coming inside is only cupboard love. What they really like is the food.

What we find, when we start looking, is that all horses (our own included) are still wild at heart. Regardless of where or how they are born and raised, all the natural instincts of the wild horse are still intact, hard-wired into the psyche. It is wild-horse instinct that makes the horse rear, buck, bolt and all the rest of what we call 'problem behaviour'.

At the same time, it is wild horse instinct that makes the horse gentle,

Horses do what their instinct tells them to do.

obedient and easy to handle. In the wild, the youngster learns from a very early age how to do as he's told and cooperate. The survival of the group or herd depends on it. Given the right environment, our own horses are no different. It is their wild-horse nature that is the essence of what makes a horse a horse, and thus not adopt the characteristics of a completely different creature.

We ask a lot of the horse. His perfect life is to roam free in a group or herd, across his familiar territory and without any human interference. There are always dangers and no vets on call, but the wild horse simply takes what comes, good, bad or indifferent. Given the choice, all horses would spend their time roaming and grazing and stopping at intervals to take a nap. The wild horse is the happiest, most contented horse on the planet. Psychologically, our own horses are no different. In their minds, they are all wild horses at heart.

What do we do? We take him away from almost everything that is normal and natural, the things that keep him happy and contented, get on his back and ask him to do all sorts of things he wouldn't dream of doing by himself. The only reason he does them at all is because of his remarkable capacity for cooperation.

Cooperation is intrinsic to the basic nature of every horse, whether born in the wild or not. All a horse ever wants is harmony. Imagine his distress when he is faced with the opposite; the one thing he hates the most – conflict. Every nerve in his body rebels against it.

All horse behaviour that we describe as undesirable is an expression of nervousness, fear or anger. We may also describe a horse as excited, but excitement often contains an element of fear. He may be 'up on his toes' or galloping around, because there is something unusual going on. He's feeling nervous, or unsure of himself.

Wild ponies doze in the midday sun.

In the wild, these expressions are part of the horse's survival kit. Most are defence mechanisms, but the horse may also attack – hence kicking and biting. As such, defensive behaviour is rarely seen in the wild. A group which is free to roam and live as Nature intended is composed of peaceful, harmonious horses. To be otherwise would be detrimental to the safety and integrity of the group. Horses have no use for aggressive/defensive behaviour, other than to avoid or escape from danger. Peaceful cooperation is paramount to their survival.

Behavioural difficulties either come singly, as in 'My horse rears', or more commonly, in multiples, as in 'He fidgets when I tack him up, won't stand still for mounting, then tries to buck me off.' The answer, as often as not, is for us do the opposite of what we were doing before.

No matter how bad the behaviour, there is always a way to bring him back to normal. All we have to do is find the way. That is the purpose of this book.

1. FIRST, UNDERSTAND THE HORSE

Despite centuries of domestication, *all* our horses still have all the instincts and desires of the wild horse. It is the baseline of all horse behaviour, whether born wild, or 'in captivity'. The horse who spends the first three years of life roaming freely in a group or herd and living as Nature intended has no confusion in his mind. He has found his identity. He knows what it means to be a horse. There is nothing dysfunctional about him at all. Our own horses have exactly the same potential.

Horses are entirely instinctual. They do not go to school and get an education. They learn from experience and live by their wits – or instincts. Everything they do is in response to instinct. The reason they let us do anything with them is that their instinct allows, or enables, them to accept our control over their lives. Most of our horses are born 'in captivity', that's to say they are not born in the wild. People are a fact of life, as natural to their environment as cows and sheep might be. It is instinct that tells them that there is nothing to fear from people, as long as there is no pain or suffering.

Problems arise when we ask the horse to go against his instincts, without a proper introduction or preparation. Most of what we ask the horse to do would normally go against his instincts, but he also very adaptable. He can get used to almost anything that isn't directly harmful. This ability to adapt comes from his capacity for cooperation. Very early in life, he learns that cooperation gives him the easy, peaceful life, which is essential to survival in the wild. Conflict is to be avoided whenever possible.

SUMMARY
❖ All horses have the instincts and inclinations of the wild horse.
❖ All horses are intrinsically lazy.
❖ The horse who has spent the first three years of life as Nature intended is potentially the perfect riding horse.
❖ Horses learn by experience and live by their instincts.
❖ Problems arise when the horse is forced to go against his instincts.

THE RULES OF SURVIVAL
In the wild, survival is entirely dependent on unity, which means playing strictly by the rules. They are:
- Stick together. Do what the others do. Don't ask questions – just do it. A lone horse might be a dead horse.
- Follow the leader – whoever that may be at the time. This is why horses appear to 'mimic' their companion(s). If one spooks, gets excited, runs away, they all do.
- Run first, ask questions afterwards.

- Don't hang around, only to find that the monster is going to have you for dinner.
- Be suspicious/afraid of anything that looks or feels even vaguely suspicious.
- Conserve energy whenever possible. It may be needed later for an emergency.
- Do as you're told! This is essential to the emotional development of the young horse and ensures that he learns what it means to be a horse. If the group or herd is to remain united, the youngster must know proper 'horse etiquette'.

From here, we get the spirit of cooperation, with no questions asked. This is what makes the horse so trainable. He learns, almost from the day he is born, to do as he's told, or he may end up dead. There is no place for the rebel in the wild horse herd. The youngster either behaves himself, or he's out. Horses can only be united when they all follow the rules and behave the same way. There is no room for discord.

The quest to conserve energy makes horses placid and lazy. Unless disturbed or provoked, they move about slowly, in a lazy way. You only have to watch your horse (or any other) when he is loose in his field to see how true this is. He mooches about, grazing, dozing and doing what horses normally do. (There are some exceptions to this in that some horses do appear more active or playful. These are usually the more highly strung, Thoroughbred types who are, as a consequence, more sensitive and easily set off or provoked into a display of energetic activity. When left to their own devices, however, most horses behave exactly like their wild counterparts.)

Social training

At the heart of this cooperative behaviour is social training. Most of a horse's learning is by imitation, doing what the others do, but foals, like children, also push the boundaries. When they go too far, they are smartly disciplined with a swift threat gesture. The foal is warned: 'Get out of the way. Keep your distance – or else!' He sees flattened ears and a raised hind leg, or a long, snaking neck thrown in his direction. He knows what these gestures mean. Only if he is really cheeky and much too bold does he get an actual kick or bite. Next time, he is more cautious!

He learns about the pecking order and his place in it – which is right at the bottom. He finds out that the respect of his elders isn't a God-given right. He must earn it, by learning the rules of social interaction. By about three years old, his social training is complete. Now, he can live the peaceful, easy life, which is the hallmark of the wild horse – and the eternal desire of our own horses!

The peer group

An additional benefit of the wild horse herd is the peer group. All social animals (including us) benefit from growing up with others of the same age. The peer group is on the same wavelength. They are all going through the same growing-up experience and understand each other. Like other youngsters throughout the natural world, peer-group babies play together and practise their survival skills, racing around and play-fighting. None of this play is harmful. There is no intention to hurt each other. It is just part of growing up.

Sometimes, they hang out together, preferring the company of their peers to the older, more staid and boring age-group. Thus they learn how to socialise and form bonds of friendship. These bonds may not last. As the foals grow older, they become less important, but for the duration, their rough and tumble companionship plays its part on the road to maturity.

Not for nothing are these called the formative years. The growing-up experience either makes or breaks a horse. If the experience of growing up is bad enough, the horse may be emotionally scarred for life.

SUMMARY
❖ Social training starts from the day the foal is born.
❖ Discipline from his elders is the cornerstone of his development.
❖ He works his way up the pecking order by learning the code of equine behaviour.
❖ He benefits from the presence of a peer group.
❖ The growing-up experience is what makes or breaks the adult horse.

Physical and emotional development
In the wild, the freedom to roam gives him confidence in himself. He is bold across country, surefooted and nimble. He has no fear of natural hazards such as water and instinctively knows how to protect himself. He is particularly protective about his feet. If the going is too rough or rocky, he makes a detour – if it's possible – or picks his way forward cautiously. His feet, along with his legs, are his most precious commodity. Without them, all is lost. He cannot survive.

Equally, he has no fear of open spaces and will hop over an obstacle, if there is no way round it. The essence of the wild horse is to use as little energy as possible. It may be needed later, for a real emergency. This, reader, is perhaps one of the most useful things you can ever know. Every horse in the universe is intrinsically lazy. In my view there is no such thing as a horse who loves jumping, or any form of racing. It goes against every bone in his body. Just because his ears are pricked forward doesn't mean he's enjoying himself. It simply means that he is paying close attention to what's in front of him, because he would be a fool not to. Going at speed is risky enough. He could trip or stumble and fall over, which might (a) damage his precious legs or (b) and infinitely worse, turn him into a lion's dinner. As for leaping over obstacles, the risk is ten times greater. He could break a leg or kill himself. No wonder he pays close attention to what's in front of him.

This is the model, evolved over the centuries, which ensures the survival of the wild horse. In captivity, it's a different story, although they can and

Horses enjoy the lazy life.

do survive equally well. However, the survival rules of the wild horse are hard-wired into every horse, no matter where they are born and how they are raised. They are still governed by exactly the same rules and instincts.

The need for company

This means that our own horses still instinctively seek the company of others of their own kind. (No, a cat or a chicken isn't good enough for a lonely horse. Cats, chickens and other animals don't speak the same language.) They prefer to follow a leader and do what the others do. If a companion feels compelled to race, they will normally want to do what the others are doing and race too. If the companion wants to plod along slowly, he will want to plod along slowly with them. Do what the other(s) do. Don't even hesitate. Your life may depend upon it.

Running away

Horses are suspicious of anything new, strange or different (including new places) and still prefer to run first and ask questions afterwards – which explains why they sometimes become hard to handle and try to run away. They *really do* want to run away, and if we try to stop them, they start to panic. In a state of panic, we have really difficult horses who might do anything.

The lazy life

As I have said, instinctively, all horses seek the lazy life, doing as little as possible in order to conserve their energy. This is what it is to be a horse. The ideal life for our own 'captive' horses is exactly the same as that of their wild counterparts. Leave them out in a good-sized pasture, with plenty of good grass and the company of others, and they are as happy as the day is long. They don't even need a stable to be happy, although some shelter provided by a wall or hedge is appreciated. To be sure, a horse with no shelter at all from the sun, wind and rain is not a happy horse, but what they like is the choice.

These instincts are inherent in every horse. They are part of his basic nature.

SUMMARY
- ❖ The freedom to roam over open country builds confidence and develops the instinct for self-preservation.
- ❖ Natural hazards hold no fear.
- ❖ The need for company of his own kind is fundamental to a horse's development and well-being. A chicken doesn't do it!
- ❖ All horses seek the lazy life.

THE PROBLEM HORSE

When a horse becomes difficult in any way, it means quite simply that something is not to his liking. His natural, instinctive defence mechanisms come to the rescue. Everything that we call 'misbehaviour' or 'disobedience' or 'resistance' is an attempt to escape from or alleviate the situation he is in. It is the only way he has of telling us that something is bothering him. In effect, it is a cry for help.

When all is well with his world, our own horse will have all the qualities of the wild horse. He is everything we want him to be. He is placid, cooperative and does as he's told. He is so easy to ride and handle that he gives nothing but pleasure. Where he comes unstuck is when presented with a situation which he doesn't like or understand, is unfamiliar or frightening.

Things he doesn't understand include carrying his head in the vertical (what for when it's not natural or comfortable?), constant pressure on the bit (why doesn't it go away?), going endlessly round a small, enclosed space (what's the point?) and leaping over fences when there is so obviously an easy way round them – to name but a few. It is only his innate desire to please and ability to cooperate that enables him to do these things at all and this desire must be appreciated and nurtured by all riders when schooling. Doing so entails such things as making changes to his *overall* outline slowly, and avoiding over-drilling him in the school or overfacing him when jumping.

'Unfamiliar' can mean anything the horse is not used to, from the way he is ridden to what he is asked to do. New home, new rider, new places, new experience all come into the category of unfamiliar. Handled with sympathy and understanding, he can get used to such things without making too much fuss about it. But if he gets the wrong response, he becomes increasingly nervous or angry.

It is easy to assume that, just because the horse has been trained, he can do anything. We bought him as a riding horse. Don't we just get on and ride? In theory, this is true, but whether he will cooperate or not depends on many factors.

Perhaps the most significant factor is what he has actually been trained to do. Has he been trained to go beautifully round a school or arena for an hour or so at a time? To what level has he been trained? Is he still basically a novice horse, or has he been trained to Olympic standards?

Has he been trained to jump? Has he been taken to competitions to get used to all the noise and excitement?

Has he been trained to hack out? On the face of it, any horse can hack out. It's easy. All he has to do is more or less follow the straight line forward, do a bit of trotting and maybe a canter or two. What is so hard about that?

To most of our horses, raised in the type of confinement we impose upon them, hacking out can be extremely difficult. It's a scary world out there, with a myriad of sights and sounds that horses aren't used to. These are things we take for granted, because we have grown up with them, but it can be very frightening to horses who have not been taken out and about until they are adult.

Additionally, he is asked to go a long way away from his home environment, the place which substitutes for the herd and where he feels safe and secure. Even if he is newly arrived, home is where he immediately establishes his security. Just going away from home (the herd) can be scary enough in itself, never mind all the bogeys and monsters out there.

Has he been trained to hack out alone? This is the scariest prospect of all. There is no other horse there to guide him and tell him what is safe and what is not. To overcome his natural, or instinctive, fear of hacking out, he must be trained to do it – and the sooner the better. This really is a very big hurdle for the captive horse to overcome.

Imagine the scenario (improbable as it might be) of a child brought up for the first few years inside a house. This child never goes outside. Beyond what he might be able to see through the windows, he has no idea what it's like out there. Imagine his fear, the first time he is ever taken out. It would

Carrying his head in the vertical is unnatural and uncomfortable for the horse unless he is progressively and correctly schooled over time to develop true collection.

The horse's willingness to leap over a fence when there is an obvious way round it is a consequence of his desire to please.

be terrifying. All that stuff out there he's never seen before and doesn't know how to deal with. Worse still would be if the house had no windows. I'll leave the rest to your imagination!

Thus it is for the horse who is born and raised in a very confined and limited environment. He may see traffic whizzing past his field every day, but to go out there and face it, to be so close and with no means of getting away from it, is another matter entirely. The same applies to everything else out there in the big, wide world. It's all new, strange and very different – and can, therefore, be frightening.

When the horse is given his basic training, usually at around the age of three, the pattern of his later life is laid down as a solid foundation. For example, the racehorse is trained to race and nothing else. This is all he knows. He is comfortable with it and performs willingly, to the best of his ability. If this horse is suddenly expected to be a pleasure horse and go for gentle hacks (as happens all too often!) he is likely to be all at sea. No one has trained him to do it.

Equally, the performance horse who has not only been trained to compete at or near the top level, but also ridden to a very high standard, cannot turn his hoof to being an ordinary pleasure horse. He doesn't know how to do it either.

When horses go through their basic training, what they learn becomes the blueprint for their later life. The older they get, they harder they find it to move away from the blueprint. In a way, they get stuck in a rut. They can do what they were initially trained to do, but anything else is like a foreign language. They don't understand it.

The older they get, the deeper the rut they get stuck in and the harder it is to move them out of it. Instinctively, they rebel or resist. How they rebel or resist depends on what they are being asked to do, how they are asked to do it and the nature of the individual horse. Essentially, they fight back, one way or another, and thus they are labelled 'a problem horse'.

So there we have it. The horse will do whatever he was initially trained to do – as long as other conditions are right, which leads to more questions.

Has the horse been raised appropriately through the first three years of life? In this respect, horses are the same as children. It is the first three years that form or

Hacking out can be scary.

shape the adult. Children learn more in their first three years than the rest of their life put together. The same is probably true of horses. What is certainly true is that the first three years of the horse's life determine the nature and ability of the adult.

Has he been raised and handled appropriately in the early years? Is he easy and comfortable with people? Has he suffered any trauma? Was his weaning brutal? Has he been given an all-round education, or has he just been trained to go beautifully through his movements? Was the training he received sympathetic to his needs and nature? A horse can be moulded into shape by sheer determination and very little willing cooperation. He can be taught to perform mechanically, but oh boy, will he be a scaredy-cat. He will probably be afraid of his own shadow.

The greater the deprivation of his emotional needs, the less flexible, adaptable and the more difficult he is going to be. Not impossible, if one has the experience and ability to handle it, but extremely difficult for anyone else. Some top performance horses, including racehorses, are known to be quite temperamental and exhibit aggressive behaviour that most of us wouldn't want to cope with.

As we know, horses can be aggressive, but why do they kick, nip, bite and snarl at us? What have we done wrong? We give them all the fuss and attention they could possibly want. We are kindness incarnate. To find the answer, we need to go back again to natural, instinctive behaviour and how horses communicate between themselves. Wild horses rarely kick or bite, except to reprimand a cheeky youngster. The message is clear. 'Go away. Get out of my space. Leave me alone. Stop bothering me!'

If a horse bites, or kicks out at us, he's feeling threatened. Ours is to find the reason why. Mostly, it's because he doesn't like what we are doing, or the way we are doing it. Through bad experience, he may not like people generally, or he may not like us in particular. We do not fit the mould he is used to and he is unable to adapt.

Blaze biting.

SUMMARY
The horse becomes difficult when:
❖ He doesn't understand.
❖ He is uncomfortable (commonly in the mouth).
❖ He dislikes what he is being asked to do.
❖ An unfamiliar activity or situation is mishandled.
❖ He has not had the appropriate training.
❖ The behaviour/attitude of his owner/rider is inappropriate.
❖ He has suffered deprivation or abuse during his formative years.

2. CONSIDER THE RIDER

There are two sides to the horse/rider partnership. Both sides play an equal part in how the horse behaves. For example, if his rider is not up to standard, a well-trained horse will forget everything he ever learned, fall back on his natural instincts and become difficult. Equally, a novice horse will resist or fight back if the rider expects or asks too much of him. Thus, when considering why horses misbehave, we must also look at the rider.

Broadly, riders come into four categories, which might be defined as beginner, novice, experienced and professional. Each has a certain level or standard of riding. The beginner is someone in the first year or so of learning to ride.

The novice is quite confident and has a reasonable level of skill. The average pleasure rider would describe themselves as a novice and, indeed, their level of skill and ability suits their purposes.

'Experienced' is someone who has ridden for a considerable number of years and is used to riding different horses. They have probably more or less grown up at their local riding school. This rider is brimming with self-confidence and will cheerfully get on almost any horse.

The professional is one who trains horses and/or competes for a living. In terms of skill and ability, the top-level rider is at the top of the tree. As a general rule, in terms of training horses for their purposes and competing, they know what they are doing. Up there with the best of them are the Spanish Riding School and the Cadré Noir, whose levels of skill and ability are probably beyond compare.

TRAINING STANDARDS

We begin to see how the standard of the horse's basic training depends on the person doing it. Right at the top are people who train to Olympic standards. The horses they train, as well as being very well bred, will usually perform impeccably – as long as they are ridden by an Olympic rider, or someone similar. Put a beginner on such a horse's back and the relationship will fall apart within minutes. This horse has been trained to expect a very high and precise level of guidance from his rider. If he doesn't get it, he becomes confused and doesn't know what to do.

BUYING A NEW HORSE

All too often, people go to see a horse with a view to buy, but don't get the right information. They watch the current owner ride the horse. He seems very well behaved and performs well. They may or may not ride the horse themselves. They listen while the owner extols the virtues of the horse. They usually ask a few questions: 'Does he buck, rear, kick or bite?', but there is one question they don't ask: 'Is he used to a rider like me: is he familiar with my level or standard of riding?' Thus, many a beginner/novice rider buys a horse who requires a higher standard or level of ability than they possess.

A TRUE STORY

An Olympic rider trained a performance horse who didn't make the grade. The horse was very sweet natured and established at Pre-novice, ideal, thought the owner, for a junior moving up from ponies to horses. When a prospective buyer phoned, the vendor raved about how honest and genuine the horse was.

A week later, the girl arrived to try the horse. She wasn't the most experienced of riders. Within minutes the horse bucked her off. The mother was disgusted, the owner deeply embarrassed. The horse should have gone to a competent competition rider who was well established and on the way up. The girl needed a steady, reliable plod to give her the confidence to go on.

Children's ponies

This discrepancy in standards is most likely to happen with children's ponies. Obviously, the anxious parent wants something quiet, sensible and well behaved, but child riders and their ponies also come at different levels and standards. Some children are very competent. They exude confidence. Their ponies live active, varied lives, going to Pony Club, competing, hacking out and so on. These ponies feel safe and secure in their rider's hands.

To the observer, such a pony is quiet, sensible and well behaved; just what the anxious parent wants for their nervous novice. The sale is made and within a week or two, the pony starts turning into the opposite of what they thought they had bought. Without the guidance of a competent rider, the pony has lost the sense of security he was used to. The inevitable result is some form of behaviour the hapless child was not expecting.

Mismatching

There are many variations to this theme. What they all boil down to is a mismatch between horse and rider. Horses who are too big, too strong, too fast, too stubborn, as well as over-trained or insufficiently trained, go to people who are unable to cope with them. Whatever the mismatch, there is trouble in store.

LEARNING TO RIDE

The bigger problem is the way riding is usually taught. Learning to ride is relatively easy. All that is needed is a placid, amenable horse and the will to succeed. We have a natural ability to communicate with horses. Left alone with an amenable horse, we work it out, as did the first horsemen who ever sat astride a horse. With no one to teach them, they followed their own instincts and found out what worked.

Where it all goes wrong is when this natural ability is drummed out of us, as is so often the case. With the emphasis on contact and control, to which most learners are subjected, any hope of real communication is lost forever. Additionally, mechanical learning of this sensitive skill engenders more fear and nervousness than trust and confidence. A nervous rider is at an immediate disadvantage.

HUMAN FRAILTY

There is also a particular human frailty to be taken into account. It is an odd one, but seems to be part of our make-up. When we are afraid of what might happen, it's as if, for some perverse reason, our brain makes us do the very thing(s) it takes to make it happen.

For example, you are worried that the horse might bolt, so what do you do? You keep a tight hold on the reins in the hope of preventing it. The horse takes off. You keep on pulling, as hard as possible. To your horror, the horse just keeps on running (I explain this in more detail in Chapter 8). Bolting was the very thing you feared. How did that happen? You had tried so hard to prevent it.

Thus we see that the input of the rider is as significant as the nature of the horse. It takes two to tango and there is many a dance that both horse and rider would prefer to avoid. It must be believed that no horse wants to be difficult any more than his owner or rider. All he wants is a quiet life. In order to achieve this, he is happy and willing to cooperate, but can only do so if we make it possible.

SUMMARY

❖ Riders come into four distinct categories, each with their own level of skill/ability.
❖ The standard of the horse's training depends on the person doing it.
❖ Buying a new horse doesn't always reveal essential information about that horse.
❖ Riders need horses who have been trained, or are accustomed to, their level of ability.
❖ Horses need riders whose level of ability matches the standard of training they have received.
❖ Children in particular need ponies who are suited or accustomed to their level of ability.
❖ The way riding is usually taught is not conducive to good communication with any horse.
❖ The input of the rider is as significant as the nature of the horse.

3. THE RELATIONSHIP

Our relationship with our horses is such that we are the leaders of the herd. They take their cue from us. They are guided, and ultimately controlled, by us. Unlike their wild counterparts, our own horses do not have the freedom of choice as to what they do or don't do, where they go or don't go, or even who they mix with. Their lives are completely controlled by us, exactly as, in the wild, their lives are controlled by the herd.

Evidently then, horses don't mind having their lives controlled, but there is a proviso. The way they live and are asked to do things for us must be to their liking. If it isn't, they rebel one way or another. Within this rebellion there is either fear/nervousness or anger – sometimes a mixture of both.

From the horse's point of view, as we have found out, when he gets nervous, fearful or angry, he does what he can to escape from, or alleviate, the situation. Left alone, he sorts himself out, does what he has to do and then forgets about it. In a group or herd, he looks to what the others are doing for guidance. If none of the others is bothered, he goes back to being calm and peaceful. This tells us that in a situation he finds difficult or disturbing, he needs to be either told or shown what to do.

As the leaders and controllers of his life, we must provide that support. We must always know what to do and how to do it. The 'what to do' we'll come to later. It's 'how to do it' that is really important.

THE GOLDEN RULES

Perhaps more than anything else, the horse needs to be accepting of us as people. In a sense, we have to become an honorary member of the species. This means that we have to be as much like them as possible.

We are the leaders: we tell the horse what to do and where to go.

Be easy in yourself

Watch a horse while he is grazing, or standing about while you do a few jobs around him. He looks at peace with the world. He is easy and comfortable with where he is, and not bothered by anything. He likes to live life in the slow lane. And this is what he likes from those around him, be it other horses, dogs or people. If there is any kind of stimulation, any tension or excitement in his vicinity, he picks it up in a flash and is immediately on the alert, ready for anything.

What we want to transmit to the horse is that same sense of easiness and not being bothered by anything. Like attracts like. The horse feels safe in our company. If he is in distress for any reason, he needs our calm sense of purpose even more. Like the support he gets from others of his own kind, he needs us to be there for him. There is no more calming influence than a quiet, self-assured presence.

Inner stillness

There is a place inside all of us that is perfectly calm, quiet and still. Horses live in this place most of the time. It gives them this air of peace and tranquillity, which is part of what makes them so lovable. Getting there is not as hard as you might think.

- Stop everything for a moment.
- Take a deep breath.
- Empty your mind.
- Tell yourself to 'Go still'.

It's amazing what you can tell yourself to do – even in the heat of the moment. And the more you do it, the easier it gets, until finally, you don't have to think about it. You are also there all the time.

What does it feel like?

Here is a very easy exercise. When your horse is contentedly doing what he likes doing best, which is either munching hay or quietly grazing, make yourself comfortable somewhere close by. Put yourself in a corner and lean against the stable wall, or lean over the fence or gate. Or you can just sit in the field. Whatever you do, you must be comfortable.

Now watch the horse munching. Listen to the gentle sound of chewing hay or cropping grass. Watch how he tears out a mouthful of hay, or collects a mouthful of grass, before chewing it, then taking another one. It can be quite mesmerising. Completely forgetting the rest of the world and all its pressures, rushing and worry, you find your inner stillness. It's that peaceful place inside, where all is still, calm and quiet.

Horses are like this all the time. You see it most clearly when they are out grazing. They mooch about, tearing at grass and nothing in the world is bothering them. Unless disturbed, everything they do is done lazily.

Much can be learned by watching.

Move like a horse

Horses never rush or hurry unless provoked, either by us, or some external influence. They take their time over everything they do. Again, we take our cue from, or are guided by, the horse. We must be slow and lazy in our movement and actions. This doesn't mean moving about like a snail, but having a quiet sense of purpose.

Forgive and forget

Sometimes we lose our temper of course. It's only human. We get annoyed, or frustrated. But horses do too. They have moments when something upsets or disturbs them, so they do accept a momentary lapse. That's OK, as long as afterwards we go back to normal.

When the horse is momentarily annoyed, scared or startled, he deals with it in the way that suits him best, then forgets about it and goes back to what he was doing before. If it's something we have done that displeases him, he will 'forgive and forget' as soon as the incident is over – as long as we have given him the right response. Like the horse then, when an incident is over and dealt with, we carry on as if nothing has happened. This is the way of the horse, and the more like the horse we can be, the better we communicate.

Think like a horse

This is a phrase that is often bandied about, but what does it mean exactly? It means to see the world from his point of view – and verbalise it. If the horse could talk, what would say? He is, in fact 'talking' to us all the time. Every minute of the day, he is telling us what he is thinking and feeling. He does it with the way he behaves. We know by looking whether he is happy, sad or mad – but there is far more to his thinking and feeling than these broad outlines. He might be saying, 'I don't like doing this. I want to go home,

Mum.' Or, 'I wish you wouldn't do that. It makes me very uncomfortable.' When we see the world from his point of view, we become soft and receptive, which is the only way we can ever communicate – and communication is the name of the game.

Show no fear

As soon as we show the horse we are fearful, we transmit this fear to the horse. Either he becomes fearful or nervous himself, or he takes advantage. 'Aha', he says, 'I'll soon put you in your place!'

You might think it's easier said than done to show no fear, but actually it isn't so hard. It's an act. We act 'as if' we have no fear. Again, we simply tell ourselves what to do. Inner stillness plays its part here. When we are in a place of inner stillness, we do not show fear. We may feel as if we should be trembling in our boots – but it doesn't show.

Don't make an issue out of it

I cannot stress this strongly enough. The more we plug away at something that isn't working, the more the battle becomes embedded in the horse's mind. We either have to find another way or leave it and try again later. Conflict gets right to the heart of the horse and lights his fire. The best way to put the fire out is to do something else.

THE LAST WORD

There is only so much that can be conveyed in words. How hard is a pull? How strong is a squeeze or kick? What exactly is 'gently, but firmly'? We can only find out by trial and error, feeling our way forward, until we get it just right. It only takes a moment or two of experimentation. We know when we've got it right, because we get the right response.

SUMMARY

The Golden Rules are:
❖ Be easy in yourself.
❖ Cultivate 'inner stillness'.
❖ Move like a horse.
❖ Forgive and forget. Carry on as if nothing has happened.
❖ Think like a horse.
❖ Show no fear.
❖ Don't make an issue out of anything.

4. THE HORSE IS NOT A MACHINE!

The horse does not do what we want just because he is a horse and that's what horses do. Almost all the things we ask of him are alien to his basic nature. They go against his wild-horse instincts, which, as we have learned, are still intact. We put him in a very small, enclosed space (stable) and expect him to stay there on his own, for long hours at a time. We tie him up and expect him to stay there while we fiddle about with him. We put a saddle and bridle on and expect him to carry us on his back.

Furthermore, when on his back, we ask him to do things he wouldn't dream of doing on his own. We ask him to go at speed and use his precious energy, when there appears to be no danger and nothing is chasing him. We ask him to sail over obstacles that he would always avoid, if possible.

We also ask him to carry himself in what to him is a most peculiar way, which includes him having his neck nicely arched and head held in the vertical. (In fact, many riders focus almost exclusively, but wrongly, on this head-carriage.) This makes no sense to him at all. He only ever does this by himself when he is really excited – and then not for long. Holding himself in this position makes his neck and back muscles ache. He is only really comfortable when he carries himself as he chooses, usually with a long, low, outstretched neck and head held more or less at a 45° angle. (This is why skilful, considerate riders introduce changes of outline slowly, and give their

Sailing over obstacles he would prefer to avoid is not the horse's idea of fun.

horses plenty of opportunity to stretch and rest their muscles.)

These alien demands we make of the horse are all things that he is perfectly entitled to rebel against, yet we have a tendency to take a very dominant position. We fix in our minds what we want and expect the horse to do it. If he doesn't, we get annoyed, frustrated, nervous or upset. Sometimes, we get frightened, when the horse does something entirely unexpected. He rears, or bucks, or gallops uncontrollably towards the horizon. A vicious circle is about to set in, as both horse and rider fall into their instinctive and conflicting reactions.

The only way to break out of the circle is to do something different. The horse is the follower. He can only do what is asked, or else react against it. He may be big, strong and powerful and appear to have a mind of his own, but in our hands, he is influenced entirely by us. It is a case of 'action and reaction'. Whatever we do, he responds to it – be it good or bad. If we get the response we want, our actions have been correct. If we get a bad response or reaction, it is because we have given him no choice.

FEARS AND PHOBIAS

We must also remember that horses are subject to their own dislikes, fears and phobias. There is no such horse as one who doesn't have them. Even at the highest level, horses may throw in a tantrum, saying, 'I don't want to play any more!' as they rear in the middle of a dressage test or 'I really don't like doing this', as they buck their way round a course of jumps. I've seen it happen at the highest level of competition where you would think the horse would know better.

However, watching how professional riders handle these little tantrums is a salutary experience. In essence, they just sit it out. We see their inner stillness like a shining light. Rarely do we see a professional rider looking flustered. Their attitude is one of acceptance. This is what the horse is doing now. Deal with it, with a minimum of fuss, then carry on as if nothing has happened. Of course, with long years of experience, they get the handling just right – and this is the tricky bit. What exactly do we do, when the horse is, from our perspective, misbehaving? There are several things we need to know.

Reading the signs

The first thing we need to do is read the signs. They tell us what the horse might be saying, if he could use our language of words. Primarily, we need to recognise the first signs of anxiety, tension and so on. These are warnings. They tell us that worse may follow, if we don't do something about it now. If not warnings, they are indicators that the horse needs our sympathy and understanding.

Anxiety:	Unable to stay still, fidgeting, pawing the ground, calling, trying to get back home or to companions. Ears move in all directions.
Tension:	Stiffness, raised head, hollow back, ears either backward or flicking about.
Nervousness:	Speediness, jogging, pulling, spookiness, hard to handle, excessive dunging, often loose. Ears may be pointed sharply forward, or back.
	NB: Anxiety, tension and nervousness are often connected.
Irritation:	Head-shaking/tossing, tail swishing, nipping, threatening to bite. A raised hind leg, ears flattened.
Anger:	Bucking, kicking, biting, flattened ears.
Rage:	Bronco bucking, vicious kicking, flattened ears.

We ignore these signs at our peril. In short, we must be as sensitive to our horse's body language as he is to ours.

On the other side of the coin are the signs that the horse is comfortable and relaxed. He is calm and easy to handle. He does what is asked without making a fuss about it. He is giving his willing cooperation. When working with a problem horse and we see these signs, we know that we are on the right track. We also know that this may not last – but that's another story!

MAKING CHANGES

First of all, when the horse's behaviour acts as a warning sign, the approach, or the way he is handled, must change. Whatever you were doing before, as a general rule, you do the opposite. Where you are over-controlling, you give more freedom. Where you are tough and determined, you soften up. Where you are too soft and letting him get away with murder, you toughen up. And where he has been spoiled in the past, you may even get angry and shout at him.

As soon as there is a change of approach, wild-horse instinct kicks in again. At first, he is suspicious. He is no longer sure of himself. There was a certain, perverse comfort in the predictability of his rut. He was used to it and, as we have learned, horses feel comfortable with what they know.

Again, depending on the nature of the problem, he may actually have difficulty in accepting the change. In this case, we do not expect to get straight to the desired end result – also known as 'end-gaming'. We simply look for improvement – which is another way of reading the signs. Any little thing he does better than before is a sign of progress. The penny is slowly dropping. Following the natural course of the wild-horse learning process, he is getting used to it. The message is getting through. What we then find is that the improvement increases into larger chunks until, finally, the new way of going is accepted and the problem disappears altogether.

The 3 Cs or the magic of three

When the horse is learning something new, be it for the first time, as in basic training, or in a process of re-education, he goes through three very specific stages, which may be referred to as the 3 Cs. I also call it 'The Magic of Three' because the effect of it can be magical.

1. Confrontation. The horse meets the change for the first time. If, according to his book of rules, it's reasonable, he will give it his best shot. Remembering, however, the comfort of the known and familiar, his best shot may not amount to much. Or he may think, 'This is OK, but can I trust it?'

2. Consolidation. The horse comes to terms with, or gets used to, what he was asked to do last time. He is still not entirely sure about it, but as long as no harm comes from it, he'll go along with it. Consolidation may just last for a day or two, or it may take a few weeks.

3. Confirmation. The lesson is assimilated and filed away for future use. As long as there is visible improvement each time, we know we are on the right track (reading the signs!). If it takes too long and the horse does not appear to be making any progress, we must think again. Overfacing does not just apply to jumping. We can just as easily overface a horse by asking for or expecting too much.

If we are lucky, the change in dynamic between horse and rider has a magical effect. The horse heaves a sigh of relief and says, in effect, 'Thank heavens for that. My voice has been heard!' Miraculously, he changes overnight – but we must never count on that. More commonly, it takes several days, even weeks to bring about this transformation.

The 3 Cs apply equally to the way adverse behaviour is fixed. We make a mistake, or error of judgement. This is the Confrontation – which indeed, it usually is. The second time we make the same mistake consolidates the experience. The horse thinks to himself, 'Aha, so this is how it works. I get scared and my rider tries to force me.' The third time is the Confirmation. 'OK, I've got it', thinks the horse. Action and reaction are now fixed into place. In other words, three repetitions of the same mistake and we are stuck with the consequences.

Horses are very forgiving by nature. If we make one mistake, or error of judgement, realise what we've done and correct it, he will 'forgive and forget'. Repeat the mistake a second time and he's worried about it, but is still able to 'forgive and forget'. It's the third time that does the damage. This is the last straw. The response is fixed in his mind.

Get the timing right

When to make a move? When not to make a move? When to ask for more? When to stay where we are? When to stay still and do nothing? These are questions that have no fixed answer. We read the signs, watch his body language and feel our way forward. If we try to push on, or ask for more before he is ready, he rebels. If we wait too long, he gets to thinking, 'That's it then. I don't have to give any more', and is harder to move on later. We can think of it a bit like working a yo-yo. If we don't get the timing between the drop and upward flick just right, we lose it. Effectively, the horse is as finely balanced as the yo-yo.

There are times when the horse is hanging in what feels like a very delicate balance. Will he, won't he, do what I want? He is thinking about it. He wants to cooperate. He hesitates. He's not sure whether to trust his rider or his instincts. At this point, we have to know the individual horse. Some

There are times when the horse is hanging in the balance.

may respond to a very definite push. Others need to be left to make up their own mind, with a nudge at exactly the right moment. Push too hard, and he backs off. If we are too soft, he just says, 'No thanks! Not today.' Once again, we must be as sensitive to the individual horse as he is to us.

Back to basics

When the horse is so nervous that much of his behaviour has got out of hand, he may need to go right back to basics and be treated as if he has never been ridden. What this does is restore the horse's confidence, by 'overwriting' all the bad stuff. As the horse has been through basic training once already, he should come to it quite quickly and easily.

BE A GOOD LEADER

When worried, or fearful, horses take their cue from those around them. Thus, the youngster looks to his elders for guidance in a stressful situation, while mature horses act collectively. Within a stressful situation, our role is to take the position of a mature, adult horse as an honorary member of the

FROM MY CASE BOOK

Pudsie (far left) had not been easy to load when she first arrived but was soon trained out of her fear and subsequently had never been a problem. Dibley, her son, had never had a problem in his life. On one occasion loading Pudsie and Dibley did, unexpectedly, turn into a bit of a nightmare. Some months later, I wanted to load them again but knew they would be deeply suspicious and unwilling.

I also knew that I would probably be able to persuade them up the ramp without too much difficulty. We had had them long enough to know each other well. Pudsie however, was likely to run out backwards as soon as I left her to go and shut the ramp and she would take Dibley with her.

There was no point in tying them up. Both were likely to fight furiously to free themselves thus turning it into another bad experience. The answer lay in bribery. Once they got their heads down into a bucket, they should be happy enough to stay there on their own for the thirty-odd seconds it would take to nip round and close the ramp.

Keeping it all very calm and normal, I led them out of the field and presented them to the ramp. As I thought she would, Pudsie suddenly got wild-eyed and nervous. And if Puds wasn't going in there, neither was Dibley.

A quiet little 'stop and wait' at the bottom of the ramp, followed by a gentle tug on the lead-rope, got Pudsie moving cautiously forwards. Acting as the leader and showing by example, I walked into the trailer and allowed Puds to follow. Dibley just came too. Where one of them goes, so does the other. Then Dibley spotted the bucket placed judiciously about halfway along the floor and surged forward. All fear now forgotten, he plunged his head into it and started munching carrots. Pudsie was more cautious but I just stood quietly, did nothing and waited until she felt it was safe to start eating too.

I stood a little while longer until both seemed completely absorbed and settled and then nipped out of the jockey door and round the back to close the ramp. It worked like a charm.

On the return journey, I repeated the same procedure just to reinforce the good experience. The next time, I used the bucket again on the outward journey as a reminder that they had nothing to fear. Knowing that they would be pleased to go home and that the memory of the past bad experience was receding, I was fairly sure that they would load without the need for bribery. And so they did. There was now no further need for bribery. The bad experience was 'forgiven and forgotten' and both ponies returned to normal.

species. We must show by example and be calm and confident about it.

When he is nervous or fearful, we must show that there is nothing to fear. We must stay grounded and solid as a rock. Our instinct may be to go for soothing reassurance, but this is only entering into the fear. By soothing him, we are saying, 'Yes, I know it's frightening', which is precisely what the fearful horse does NOT want to hear. He needs to be told, 'Don't be so daft, it's only a rock' (or whatever it is).

Voice control

Horses are as sensitive to sound as anything they see. The voice therefore can be a useful tool, but the tone must be pitched just right. A high, squeaky voice is perceived by the horse to be like a mouse and not worth listening to. Too strong a voice may be deafening. A scream is frightening, not least because a scream comes from a frightened person, who instantly transmits that fear. A good, loud shout, on the other hand, may serve a useful purpose.

It may be used to cut through fear in certain situations, rather like a slap to a hysteric. When the horse is panicking, a loud, sharp 'Whoaaa' may help to some extent. If nothing else, it makes us feel better – and the better we feel, the better for the horse.

Equally, a momentary loss of temper may cut through the shenanigans of a spoilt horse and bring him to his senses. This, however, only applies to horses who are trying it on because, in the past, they have always got away with it. Again, we have to know the individual horse. Applied to the wrong horse, or at the wrong time, shouting merely serves to increase his fear.

We can think of the voice as a useful accessory. We can manage perfectly well without it. Our actions and body language tell the horse everything he needs to know, so when in doubt, say nothing!

Body checking

This is such a useful tool, particularly when riding, although the principles apply equally well on the ground. I use it all the time, even now. When the going gets tough, our own natural instincts make us tense up. Everything tightens, from head to toe. When we get tense, what happens to the horse? He gets tense and anxious too.

Above all, I want to be sure I am not doing anything which might make a bad situation worse. As soon as I feel a horse tense up, I do a quick body check, to make sure I am not adding to it. I start with my feet and legs. Are they soft, relaxed and in the right place, which is straight down, underneath my body? Am I gripping, when I shouldn't be? I then move my attention up to my body. Is it upright, or am I leaning too far forward? Is my neck soft and relaxed, or is it rigid with tension? Is my head above my shoulders, or has it tipped forward or back?

Body checking can be done in a second or two, is always worth the effort and is particularly useful when the horse starts getting difficult. The way to get used to the idea is to practise when you are going along smoothly. Just focus your attention in this order:

Feet ⟼ Legs ⟼ Body ⟼ Neck ⟼ Head

Do this several times while you are riding. Think of it as part of your 'equipment', as useful as the aids you are accustomed to. Keep practising, until it becomes second nature.

ACHIEVABLE TARGETS

Finally, we come to a most important element of working with horses, which is breaking the process down into the smallest possible parts. This provides us with targets or goals we know we can achieve. It might also be called working in baby steps or 'bite-sized chunks'.

A baby learns to walk by taking one step at a time. He does not suddenly stop crawling, get up off the floor, run around and play. He takes one or two tentative steps, and then loses his balance. Undaunted, he tries again and slowly but surely puts more steps together, until he is walking properly. Without realising it, he sets himself achievable targets, each one taking him a little further on.

Similarly, when working with horses, we ask for one small step at a time, which we know is achievable. Sometimes, as with leading problems for example, it is literally only one step to begin with, but success builds on success. By achieving a succession of very small goals, we reach the desired end result. As each task is so small, the horse gets to thinking 'Yes, I can do this'. The more he thinks 'I can do this' and finds it easy and comfortable, the more his confidence grows. Slowly, we build both his confidence and ability.

This principle applies not just to resolving problems, but also to avoiding creating them. For example, if you want to teach a horse to jump, it's no use trotting him over poles on the ground, then asking to jump a course of 0.9m (3ft) fences. He will simply say, 'I won't! I haven't been prepared for this' and that will be the end of his jumping career.

If we do make an error of judgement and ask for too much, the horse will let us know immediately with a resistance in one form or another. If this happens, we think, 'Oh dear, I shouldn't have done that. I've pushed him too hard. I'd better go a bit easier next time.'

What we must bear in mind is that we do not *expect* to get to the desired end result immediately. With some behaviour, this can be achieved, but more often than not, changing behaviour is a more of a process than an instant miracle. We expect only to achieve a succession of goals or targets, which eventually arrive at the ultimate goal.

Of course, we keep the ultimate goal in mind. We know what we are aiming for and this helps to determine what the achievable targets should be. For example, we want a horse to stop moving away while we are mounting, so the first achievable target is just to get him to stand still … and so we go on, one small success at a time, until he stands quietly and obediently for mounting.

Make it easy

On the bottom line, all horses are born to cooperate. The desire to please is embedded in the basic nature of every horse. Even in the worst behaved, the desire to please is still there. It's just a question of finding the way to get to it. Better still, the way to do it is simple. Make it easy for your horse to do what you want. The trick may be to lower your expectations so that what's easy for the horse becomes easy for us too. What a bonus!

THE EFFECT OF BAD EXPERIENCE

There are times when, with all the will in the world, things go wrong. We make an error of judgement, or we may just be in a bad mood. What should have been easy turns into an all-round bad experience. What happens for the horse is that the next time he faces the same situation, he will be fearful. He will have completely forgotten that, before the unpleasant incident, he no problem at all. What we have to do now is recognise his fear and treat him accordingly.

SUMMARY
- ❖ All horses have fears and phobias.
- ❖ Read the signs and act accordingly.
- ❖ Use the 3 Cs to gauge progress.
- ❖ Get the timing right.
- ❖ Go back to basics, if necessary.
- ❖ Be a good leader.
- ❖ Voice control is a useful accessory.
- ❖ Turn body checking into a habit.
- ❖ Work with achievable targets.
- ❖ All horses are born to cooperate.
- ❖ Make it easy for the horse to do what you want.
- ❖ What's easy for him is easy for us too.
- ❖ Bad experience can be 'forgiven and forgotten' by turning it into a pleasant one.

PART 2
DEALING WITH PROBLEMS UNDER SADDLE

This part of the book is all about problems in the ridden horse, and how to make it easy for your horse to do what you want. We will see that what might be considered 'front line' problems – rearing, bucking, bolting – usually arise as responses to excessive restraint, coercion or force. But what happens when none of these things *appears* to be excessive, but is too much for the individual horse?

We have discovered that horses are both tolerant and adaptable. They can and do put up with a lot, so much so that we make assumptions. The biggest assumption we make is that they will all do what we want, without making a fuss about it – and without exception. We have been taught how to ride. They have been taught how to be ridden. Isn't that the end of it?

What tends to be forgotten is that horses' training and experience is so different. Even their basic training varies from one trainer to another. Many wind up going through several different homes and the experience of each can be very different. While it might legitimately be claimed that a horse can work in the school and hack out – alone or in company – *how* he is used to doing these things is open to question.

Such a varied experience makes horses sensitive. Their tolerance level drops. Everything has to be just right for the individual horse in order that he can behave as he should. And what is just right for one horse is not necessarily right for another.

Thus, one horse responds to a bit of welly to make him go forward: another will not stand for it. One horse will tolerate rein and/or leg contact on a happy hack out: another dislikes it. One horse likes strong direction and guidance from his rider: another prefers none at all and will plod along happily doing his job, answering only to the simple aids and doing it very well.

Unfortunately for the horse, there is a tendency to believe that 'one size fits all'. Whatever we have been taught to do, we expect the horse to respond correctly to it. When he doesn't, or does something awkward or unexpected, we are mystified. Why is he doing that?

One particular issue is that most horses these days are trained to be ridden on a rein contact, but the question arises – how much? Are you actually pulling on the horse's mouth and making him uncomfortable? If you are, he lets you know in a variety of different ways.

The other side of the coin from putting too much pressure on horses is not giving enough clear guidance. Thus, in addition to suffering from too much coercion or restraint, horses can also suffer from lack of discipline. This leads them to be pushy and very resistant. In the wild, foals are disciplined from a very early age. This is how they learn to be obliging and cooperative. Between horses themselves, discipline is clear and precise. We need to follow their example.

5. REARING

Rearing comes in many shapes and sizes. There are rears, which are described as vertical, when the horse rears up as high as his balance will allow. At the other end of the scale is little more than a bunny-hop, where the forefeet are just lifted off the ground. In between is a range of medium rears, all of which bear the same characteristic. For whatever reason, the horse doesn't want to go forward.

The two colts in the photo are practising their stallion skills. They go up on their hind legs to make themselves look bigger and more intimidating. This behaviour is hard-wired into every horse, but, given the opportunity, it is young colts in particular who practise by play-fighting. They mean no harm and don't hurt each other. It's just a game!

Foals play-fighting.

ORIGINS OF REARING – A BLOCKING MECHANISM

Here lies the origin of rearing. It is a blocking mechanism, intended to intimidate an adversary and, in the wild, mostly employed by stallions. Where riders are concerned, their intimidation is usually successful. Most people find rearing quite terrifying.

So why do our horses rear? They have no need to fight for supremacy. We make sure of that. People say, 'My horse rears for no apparent reason.' But

HORSE FACT

Rearing used to be considered (and often still is) a vice. The implication is that the horse is vicious, mean-spirited, evil-tempered. Nothing could be further from the truth. Like any other behaviour, any horse can and may rear, if provoked. It is merely the horse's instinctive reaction to a situation which offers him no other way out.

My theory is that it is the image of the wild stallion, rearing up in combat with another, which has provoked this myth. Of course, the wild stallion is merely defending his position as master of his mares. Such challenges are few and far between. Most of the time, the wild stallion is as gentle as a pussy-cat.

there is always a reason, and the bigger the rear, the bigger the reason – and the reason is simple. They have been provoked into feeling the need to block forward movement and, if possible, intimidate.

From the horse's point of view, no horse wants to rear. All he wants is a quiet life, like that of his country cousins. He doesn't want to be aroused, or provoked. It means that something bad is happening. He is being asked to do something that goes against his instincts, but his rider has other ideas. Instinctively, the horse tries to block it. The horse and rider are now in conflict. The horse doesn't like that either. The essence of solving the problem of rearing, as is so often the case, is to remove the conflict. First, however, we must put the rearing into the right context.

EXCESSIVE FORCE

When we pull against the horse, we create an instant conflict. Whatever we want from him, he wants the opposite. For example, you want to load your horse into a lorry or trailer. He doesn't want to go in there and stops at the bottom of the ramp. You pull on the rope. He pulls back against you. If you continue pulling, he will rear up in an attempt to free himself. This may or may not be successful. If he does get free, he will run away as his first line of defence.

For the horse, the prospect of going into the small, enclosed space of a lorry or trailer is frightening. This is a natural fear which is directly connected to his wild-horse instincts. It is the fear of entrapment. From his point of view, once trapped, anything could happen. In his mind, whatever happens can only be bad. Concerned only for his own safety and well-being, fear overwhelms his desire to cooperate.

In this situation (as with so many others!) the main objective is to remove the conflict and persuade the horse that no harm comes from entering this space. There are several ways to do it – see Chapter 16 for more detail.

SUMMARY
❖ Excessive force creates conflict, which the horse attempts
    to resolve by pulling away/rearing.
❖ Fear overwhelms the desire to cooperate.
❖ The first objective is to remove the conflict.

EXCESSIVE RESTRAINT

Excessive restraint comes into much the same category as excessive force. There is too much of it. Again, horse and rider are in conflict. This can happen on the ground, when leading or when the horse is tied up, but most commonly, this happens when riding. The horse wants to go forward, but is restrained by a strong hold on the reins.

From the horse's point of view, there is the discomfort of too much pressure in his mouth. He wants to get rid of it. He may also want to run away – very fast. He is fired up. He wants to go, but his rider says no, so he rears. The more fired up the horse and the stronger the hold on the reins, the bigger or higher the rear.

WHAT I WOULD DO

This does depend on the situation but, primarily, I would seek to avoid excessive restraint or pressure on the horse's mouth. I would start with a body check to ensure that I have absolutely no leg contact, as this also encourages the horse to rear. If he is raring to go, but needs to be slowed, I would first take quite a sharp pull, to tell him that I want him to slow down. Then I would release the reins, just enough to give him the space to respond. The duration of a couple of strides is just about right. Then, I would take another pull and release the pressure again … and keep on doing that, until he gets the message and does what I want.

I call this action 'give and take' on the reins. In dressage terms, it's 'give away and re-take the reins'. Having started with a pull, I let the reins go (give them away) and then take them back again. Doing this makes the signal to slow down very clear and enables the horse to understand what is wanted. In the adjacent photo sequence, I demonstrate the subtlety of 'give and take' on the reins.

'Give and take': take a pull, then release the pressure.

As I take a pull, the horse's neck appears to shorten. This shows that the horse has felt the pressure and 'heard' what I am saying. On the release, the neck lengthens in a moment of softening. It is in this moment of softening that he has the opportunity to respond to the 'slow down' signal of the pull.

When the horse you are riding is fired up and raring to go, you have to repeat this little procedure several, if not many, times, but each time you should feel a slight reduction of his energy level until finally, you get what you want. You then reward the horse by releasing the reins and letting him have his head. A pat on the neck won't come amiss either!

It is the constant pressure that makes the horse rear. He can't get away from it. He doesn't know what else to do. He is also bursting with energy. It has to go somewhere. 'Give and take' on the reins gives him a signal or message he can understand, without the unrelenting pressure in his mouth which makes him want to run away.

When we want him to stand still
Sometimes the horse rears when he wants to go and we want him to stand still – to cross the road, for example, or at the start of some kind of race.

WHAT I WOULD DO

Again, what I would do depends on the situation, but a quick body check always comes first. The following example, and the accompanying photos, show how I would deal with a horse who doesn't want to stand still when crossing a road.

First, I try 'give and take' on the reins to persuade him to wait where he is. I prepare for this by starting the process a little in advance, so that by the time we get to the kerb, he has got the message.

Failing this, and if there is room, I make small circles to allow him forward movement, asking for halt each time we come back to the appropriate position. If he declines to halt, I

Trying a 'give and take' on the reins.

would keep circling. This does make watching the traffic for a space to cross that much more difficult, but happily for us, we can rotate our heads and keep looking.

Making small circles. *Dismounting to hold the horse and lead him in hand.*

More often than not, if I know the horse is going to be difficult, I simply dismount and hold him. It's a bit of a hassle, because I have to get on again, but it is by far the easiest method and usually works like a charm. It is so much easier to control the horse from the ground than when mounted.

At first, the horse may still fidget. He's anxious. He needs to move, but that's OK. A little fidgeting does no harm to anyone. All I need to do is prevent him from going forward across the road, which really isn't so difficult. Otherwise, he can more or less do what he likes. And as long as I am not hanging onto the reins for dear life, he definitely won't rear.

Thus my advice is that, beyond ensuring that your horse does not surge forward without you, take no notice of what he does, perform your usual road-drill and lead the way across it when the road is clear. By going out in front, you show by example and act as leader. Give him the freedom to follow and he almost certainly will.

HORSE FACT

Horses are instantly reassured when the rider dismounts. Immediately, they have one less thing to worry about. The effect is often magical, although it may not solve the problem entirely. Where there is fear or lack of confidence, this must still be addressed. However, with our feet firmly on the ground, we (a) have much more control and (b) can be more persuasive. Remembering that horses are prone to following the leader and doing what the others do, on the ground, we are in the best possible position to show by example.

Training by doing

There is no better way to train a horse than by experience. We can spend as much time as we like training him to stand and wait at home in the school or arena, but out on a ride, or in another place, the situation is entirely different. Other factors come into play.

I call this 'training by doing'. In the situation just described, I am showing by example that when I dismount the horse stops. Horses are already familiar with this idea, except that it is usually associated with ending a ride – but they can learn that it applies anywhere.

The great day comes when I realise that I don't have to dismount any more. The horse has understood that when we come to a traffic situation, he stops and waits until I tell him to go on. A gentle 'feel' on the reins is all that is needed.

HORSE FACT

Although some horses may see certain types of traffic as 'scary objects', horses have no concept of the general danger of traffic. The horse's instinct is to simply go where he wants to go, at whatever speed suits him and let the traffic take care of itself. This is why it is often so difficult to convince the horse that he must stop and wait for it to pass.

Formal training

Training your horse to stand still can also be done formally. You can do it on your own, using the 'give and take' on the reins technique, combined with a strong voice command. Easier by far, however, is to enlist the help of a handy assistant.

Your handy helper stands directly in front of the horse (to physically block his forward movement) and takes a *light* hold of the bit-rings. The purpose here is not so much to restrain the horse as to *suggest* that he stays where he is. A very light, backward pressure can be applied if necessary, but most horses understand by the physical block in front of them that they should stay where they are.

Training the horse formally to stand still.

Meanwhile, you summon your inner stillness, sit very quietly and show by example what you want. As the horse understands what is wanted, your handy helper backs away one step at a time. To put the training to the test, walk about a bit and ask for halt in the usual way. As he comes to halt, relax the rein, go still and sit quietly. At first, your helper may need to step in. Remembering the Magic of Three, your horse should soon get the idea.

NB: If the horse is very fidgety, you can also use bribery. Instead of your helper holding the bit-rings, they drip-feed little treats. This horse may, however, take longer to get the idea.

Starting a race

Rearing at the start of a race or similar competition is most likely to happen to children with ponies when doing gymkhana games. The pony knows what's coming, is all fired up and raring to go. He has no concept of 'starter's orders'. He just wants to go, is heavily restrained and rears.

In this situation, I would ask someone to hold the pony on the starting line. This may be a bit demeaning for the rider, but do they want to stop the pony rearing or not? If a handy helper isn't available, there is no choice but to sit it out – which isn't so difficult (see page 54).

EXPERT TIP

If your horse gets over-excited and very fidgety at shows, practise your standing still technique and encourage him to wait quietly. Failing all else, dismount and stand quietly with him. He may like to graze, which is no bad thing. It's comfort eating pure and simple and helps the horse relax.

SUMMARY
- ❖ Excessive restraint creates conflict, combined with discomfort or pain.
- ❖ It is the constant pressure that makes the horse rear.
- ❖ When riding, the first step is to relieve the pressure on his mouth.
- ❖ Use 'give and take' on the reins instead of constant, relentless pulling.

EXCESSIVE COERCION

By contrast to excessive restraint, the horse may also rear when urged forward too forcefully. The reins can be quite loose, meaning that it is not the pressure on his mouth that the horse is objecting to, only the forcefulness or pressure from the rider who is trying to make him go where he doesn't want to go.

From the horse's point of view, what he is being asked to do, or where he is being asked to go, is not acceptable. 'No', he says, 'I won't!' It is as if there is a scary monster in front of him, but it's invisible. There *is* a scary monster, but it's in his head. The monster is saying, 'If you go there, or do that, I'll eat you for breakfast.'

The comfort zone

Usually, this reaction concerns the horse's comfort zone, which relates to the territory of the wild horse. Inside it, or within his known and familiar territory, he feels safe and secure. Outside this area of familiarity, the world is a scary place.

The comfort zone is usually geographical. The horse will go so far, then stop and refuse to go any further. Any forceful attempt to make him go further brings his blocking mechanism into play and induces him to rear.

However, the comfort zone can also apply to what we ask him to do. Some things are comfortable and familiar. He finds them easy. Others, often relating to things like schooling and jumping, he finds hard. There comes a point when he says, 'I don't like doing this – and I won't!'

WHAT I WOULD DO
Hacking

If this occurs when out hacking, I usually dismount, without even thinking about it. Quietly, I take the reins over the horse's head. This gives him a breather and lets him know that I am not fussed about it. I then lead him forwards, taking my position as leader, by walking forwards myself. As often

If the horse feels outside his comfort zone out hacking, it may be sensible to dismount and lead him.

as not, he checks back for a moment, then follows. If he is a little unwilling, I use the 'give and take' technique.

Having shown that I am sympathetic to his fears, this usually works. (If not, the subject is discussed at greater length in Chapter 10.) I then remount and carry on as if nothing has happened.

I then consider how far I should take him outside his comfort zone. Having overcome this little block, the better part of valour is usually to turn him round and take him home. Each time I hack out, I extend his comfort zone a little more, until it embraces the whole area I want to ride in. In this way, there is no more rearing.

Schooling, etc.

Much the same idea applies to schooling, jumping, etc. A horse very rarely just stops and rears. There are almost always warning signs. He's getting fidgety. He's reluctant to go forward. He doesn't seem to be listening so well. His ears are back. His tail is swishing. Heeding these warning signs, I first do a body check, to make sure I am not provoking him. If I am confident in my position, the next option is to stop where I am. The horse is telling me he's had enough. Either I go back to doing some easier stuff, or end the session and pick up again another day. This puts an end to any thoughts of rearing.

Habituation

The responses detailed above in respect of the comfort zone are examples of 'habituation', or getting the horse used to the idea of doing something he finds difficult. When confronting a fear, he can only assimilate a very little at a time. We tend to think 'Why shouldn't he hack out for an hour?' However, from the horse's perspective, he can only manage twenty minutes. After that, he's outside his comfort zone.

We tend to think 'Why can't we progress him in his schooling?' He thinks, 'This is tedious and boring and I don't like doing it'. A little bit at a time changes everything.

The physical block

Finally, we come to refusing to go forwards because of what is in front of him. Usually, it's uncertain terrain. Horses don't much like the hollow sound of ramps and bridges, as if instinct is telling them they may not be safe. Most of them don't much like going into water. Even if it's shallow, they don't know what lies underneath it. They might get stuck in mud and find themselves trapped. Or there might be a crocodile lying in wait, although I suspect that even a horse knows this is unlikely.

Or, what lies in front of them simply looks odd and vaguely threatening. From their point of view, it is better to simply avoid going over it.

WHAT I WOULD DO

If I cannot persuade the horse to go forward with gentle insistence from the saddle, I dismount and lead him forward. To illustrate the point, in the

Leading the way and showing by example.

adjacent sequence of photos, we are demonstrating how to persuade a horse to walk over a tarpaulin.

I start by walking forwards, leading the way and showing by example. As you can see, the reins are loose. I am expecting and allowing him to follow. Copper trusts me enough to follow quietly until he gets to the point where the next step would take him onto the tarpaulin.

Then he says, 'No, I can't do this. I don't like the look of that surface.' He stops and tries to back away from it. All I want to do now is stop him from backing way from it so I maintain just enough tension on the reins to meet his resistance.

Finding he is not allowed to go backwards, he tries to go sideways in the hope of dodging round it. Maintaining the pressure on the reins to stop him going backwards, I stay very firmly grounded and watch his forefeet.

In my mind I am focused on getting his forefeet where I want them, which is in a position to take the first step onto the tarpaulin. This is a bit of a mind trick. When you try it, you must focus your attention on where you want the horse's forefeet to go and, to some extent, your mind does the rest. You find, almost unwittingly, that you are giving the horse the right signals.

Copper is now in a bit of a fix. He can't back away and now I seem to be controlling his sideways movement. He goes into a straight resistance with a very firm 'I won't!' All I do now is maintain the same pressure on the reins – and my inner stillness – and wait. If I pulled now, he would rear up. Instead, I simply stop and wait for him to submit.

Lo and behold, the penny drops. Copper has understood that there is no way out. He takes the first step onto the tarpaulin. Instantly, I release

Top: The horse tries to back away.
Middle: Finding he can't go backwards, the horse tries to go sideways.
Bottom: Straight resistance is countered by simply waiting.

all pressure on the reins. He is doing what I want and needs no further persuasion.

Having taken the plunge, I now know that Copper will go all the way. As you can see, there is no pressure on the reins at all. Having been persuaded that he could do this, Copper is following of his own free will. Nonetheless, his raised head, uncertain ears and nervously raised hind leg show that he is still not entirely sure about it.

I have made the point. No harm comes from crossing the tarpaulin. We need to go round again though, to consolidate the learning. The next time, Copper will find it easier and more acceptable.

The second time round, Copper steps onto the tarpaulin with barely a moment's hesitation. I have gained his trust completely. Look how calm and relaxed he is now. As you can see, I give him plenty of space to follow along behind me.

Now it's Chelsea's turn. She takes over and leads Copper over the tarpaulin with no trouble at all. The final objective though is to ride him over it. You might think that having been led over the tarpaulin three times, he would take being ridden over it in his stride. But this is not necessarily so. As soon as a rider gets onto a horse, the dynamics change.

Top: The penny drops: the first step forward.
Middle: Progress continues.
Bottom: The second attempt is far less hesitant.

On the ground, you will find that the horse accepts you as the leader and, once persuaded, is willing to follow. With a rider on his back, he no longer has a leader. Suddenly, he is responsible for himself. The fear he felt before comes back. 'Oh no' he says, 'I can't do that!'

Chelsea straightens Copper out. I tell her to stop and wait, sit still and do nothing. She gives him a few moments to drop his head and inspect the tarpaulin. 'Yes Copper. It's the same tarpaulin and you can do it.'

Having waited a few moments and when the time feels right, Chelsea asks Copper to walk on normally. 'OK' he says, almost cheerfully. On a nice loose rein, Chelsea rides Copper over the tarpaulin. Mission accomplished.

With no leader on the ground, the horse is once again hesitant.

Given time to consider, the horse takes the plunge.

Time taken – about twenty minutes.

It must be noted that this training is not transferable. Training your horse to walk over a tarpaulin at home doesn't mean that he will walk over anything anywhere. If you meet a strange surface or going in another situation your horse will show exactly the same suspicion. The value of the training lies in giving you the tools if or when you meet such a situation. In other words, you know what to do and how to do it.

Finding the balance

The trick when handling such blocks is to be sensitive to the horse's uncertainty. There is a fine line between too much encouragement and too little. You must feel your way forward, sensing how much the horse trusts your judgement – or not, as the case may be.

Thus, you maintain just the right pressure on him, not so much that he resists and pulls back, but enough to let him know that you are not giving up. It is a delicate balance between yes and no, which you aim to conclude in your favour.

It is not only solid objects or uncertain terrain which may provoke the horse into planting his feet and rearing. He can also have an equally solid block in his mind about what is coming next – and he doesn't like it. Mostly, this relates to hacking and schooling, comes into the general category of refusing to go forwards, and will be discussed later (Chapter 10).

HORSE FACT

Training the horse to accept uncertain terrain is not transferable. Just because we have trained him to walk over a tarpaulin (or similar) at home, in the field or paddock, doesn't mean he will go willingly over something similar elsewhere. If we train him to paddle across a stream, it doesn't necessarily mean he will go through puddles. Each situation is seen by the horse as being entirely different.

What such training does do, however, is strengthen our relationship and the horse's trust in our judgement – which of course, is no bad thing.

SUMMARY

❖ Excessive coercion is a battle of wills, which brings us into conflict.
❖ What the horse is being asked to do, or where he is asked to go, is not acceptable.
❖ The comfort zone is not only geographical but emotional as well.
❖ Techniques I would use for hacking:
  – Dismounting.
  – 'Give and take'.
  – Extend the comfort zone by degrees.
❖ Techniques I would use for schooling:
  – Watch for warning signs.
  – Either end the session or go back to something easier.
  – The physical block.
  – Dismount and lead in hand.
  – Find the balance between too much encouragement and too little.

Don't forget that such training is not transferable. Any situation is assessed by the horse on its merits.

MIXED MESSAGES

Another common cause of rearing is mixed messages. If you want to train a horse to rear, this is precisely how you do it. You take a tight, unrelenting hold on the reins and simultaneously urge him strongly forward. This gives the horse nowhere to go but up.

From the horse's point of view, he is confused. He doesn't know what to do. The reins are telling him to stay where he is, while the legs are telling him to go forward. Pressured from all sides, there is not much he can do. He rears.

Something is bothering him. Most commonly, it's what is coming next and/or his rider being over-anxious or nervous about something like an imminent competitive event. Most people feel some degree of anxiety or nervousness at the start of a competition. It's perfectly normal. Everyone wants to do well, but in your anxiety, you come on too strongly. The horse doesn't like it, so he resists, usually at the entrance to the ring.

WHAT I WOULD DO

The first thing I would do on a horse who has been confused by mixed messages is a body check. This horse really needs me to be soft and relaxed. Then I clarify the message. I remove the 'stop' signal by loosening the reins. I sit very still and do nothing for a moment or two, to let the horse draw breath and calm down. Then I politely squeeze him forward, asking nicely for him to do what I want. I might try that a couple of times, with a little break between each squeeze. It depends on how resistant he is.

If he is adamant that he is not going directly forward, I might try changing direction. Again, it depends on the situation. As a last resort, I would dismount and lead him forward, even if it means walking on foot into the ring and remounting. Most people these days are very understanding. At local-level shows, at any rate, you are likely to be allowed to lead the horse into the ring, then mount him. Depending on the rules of the competition concerned, this may affect your placing – or even lead to you having to compete hors concours – but this is a price worth paying for long-term benefit.

Objections aside, the *objective* is simple. It is to remove the fight and make it easy for the horse to go forward.

SUMMARY
- ❖ If you want to train a horse to rear, repeatedly give him strong mixed messages.
- ❖ A body check ensures the rider is relaxed.
- ❖ The first port of call is to clarify the message.
- ❖ Calm the horse by loosening the reins, sitting still and doing nothing.
- ❖ Change direction or dismount and lead.

HOW TO SIT A REAR

You simply lean forward and give away the reins. In this position, you cannot fall off. Additionally, the horse will not be unbalanced and fall over. What goes up must come down. The horse cannot stand on his hind legs for longer than a few seconds, unless he's a circus horse and trained to stay up

The position that allows a rider to sit a rear.

there for longer. In coming back down, he may rear again, but that's OK. We just sit it out.

He may or may not learn to wait patiently for the start of a race. He knows what is coming and there is so much adrenalin flowing, he may find it very difficult to stand still. If he learns to wait for the signal to go on, this is very good. If he doesn't, so be it.

REARING WHEN LEADING

From the horse's point of view, rearing when the handler is on the ground relates to the horse's fear of entrapment and/or excessive restraint. The entrapment comes from not being able to do what he wants to do and the restraint comes from the headcollar and lead-rope. In other words, the more we pull or hold him back, the more likely he is to rear.

The difficulty usually arises when the horse wants to rush off at speed. He is nervous, or over-excited. He wants to go. He's getting a rush of adrenalin. The pace is too slow. You can't keep up. You want him to slow down and walk at a normal speed. Neither do you want to let go and lose him.

WHAT I WOULD DO

Quite simply, as he tries to rush off, I would bring him round in a circle. If he is really strong, and I know what's coming, I attach the lead-rope to the side-ring of the headcollar, as this gives a really clear signal. All I do is allow him to get a very short way ahead, stand my ground and allow the rope to go taut. At this moment, the horse understands that he must turn.

Strangely perhaps, he's quite happy to do this. His primary objective is to run. Now, nothing is stopping him. He can go as fast as he likes, except that on a small circle, the best he can usually manage is trot.

Notice in the accompanying photo how the rope is actually quite loose.

If the led horse tries to rush off, bring him onto a circle.

This mare knows she can't go anywhere else, so she keeps on going round the circle, until she gets back to the starting point. One circle is usually enough but, if necessary, I would send the horse round again in exactly the same way. Notice also the handler's inner stillness as she maintains her composure and shows by example. This is really important, as it puts out a strong message to the horse: 'I'm not flapping about this and there is no need for you to flap either, so calm down and behave yourself.' All this is said just by maintaining composure.

Eventually, the horse gets tired of running round in circles and settles down to walk along quietly. If he surges forward again, I simply repeat the procedure each time, until he gives in and stops even trying (see Chapter 16 for more detail).

How long it takes him to settle is impossible to say. It depends on the level of anxiety/excitement and how far we have to take him. In any event, the essence is that his need to go faster has been accommodated without the conflict that makes him rear.

SUMMARY

❖ Rearing when leading relates to fear of entrapment and/or excessive restraint.
❖ The more he is pulled or held back, the more likely he is to rear.
❖ The answer is to make him circle round us: allow it by keeping the rope loose. There is no need to hang on while he is circling.
Repeat as many times as is necessary.

REARING WHEN TIED UP

A horse may also rear when he is tied up. He may have been startled, or simply doesn't want to be there. He pulls back to free himself and finds that he is trapped. He can't get away. At this point, he panics. Even though it is self-inflicted, we come back here to excessive restraint on the rope.

From the horse's point of view, he desperately wants to free himself. Like us, the horse cannot think clearly when he is in a state of panic. He simply reacts to his instinct, even though it may be counter-productive.

WHAT I WOULD DO

As soon as I see a horse in deep distress, my first priority is to release him immediately – if he hasn't released himself that is! In this state of panic, he is likely to do himself some damage and I don't want this to happen. I also know that leaving him to struggle turns a bad experience into a terrible one.

The problem now is that whatever the initial provocation, tying up is now associated with fear and/or panic. This means that I won't tie him up at all

If a horse tries to fight the rope when tied, simply hold it instead.

HORSE FACT

When the horse is agitated, he must be allowed to move, if only in small circles. His wild-horse instinct demands it. Only through expressing his anxiety in movement can he come to where we want him. Movement also allows some outlet for extra adrenalin, which is why it can be helpful to keep a horse moving in the start box of cross-country; walking round at a meet, etc. The more we try to restrain him, to make him do what we want, the closer we get to a conflict, which only makes a bad situation worse.

---

for a while, because the association will be instantaneous. Without thinking twice, he will panic and fight the rope.

What I do instead is simply hold the lead-rope and do what I have to do. It may be a trifle awkward. The horse may be fidgety, but again, I would keep him on a small circle around me until he gets the idea and finds that nothing is achieved by circling. (See Chapter 17 for more detail.)

SUMMARY

❖ The horse finds he is trapped and panics. He does anything to free himself, including rearing.

❖ The first priority is to release him.

❖ Subsequently, the lead-rope must be held.

❖ Re-introducing the horse to tying up must be done with caution.

❖ A relapse is always possible, in which case the procedure is repeated.

FROM MY CASE BOOK

Tequila reared every time anyone got on her back. As often as not, she fell over. Many had tried to overcome this problem. All had failed. Starting from the first time I rode her, she never reared again. Without even seeing anyone else ride her, I knew what they were all doing wrong. I knew that all I had to do was give her a loose rein (to take the pressure off her mouth) and keep my legs well away from her body.

The first time I rode her, I was body checking constantly. All I asked was for her to walk to the end of a fairly big field, turn round and go back to the gate. It was a hairy experience. I could feel this mare bunched up underneath me, ready to explode. I couldn't even steer a straight line, as I hardly dared touch the reins. Part of her was niggling to go back to the gate, where she hoped I would dismount and put her away – which is what her riders normally did, if they hadn't been thrown off already.

I knew I had to be super-sensitive about her mouth. Rearing by then was such an ingrained habit that it wouldn't take much to provoke it. Any touch to the reins had to be as light as possible. And so we kind of meandered down to the end of the field and made a large, comfortable half-circle to turn round. I sensed she wanted to bolt back to the gate, so I sat as still as is humanly possible, body checking every step of the way and let her get on with it – again without any rein pressure.

Her walk was fast and tense – but she walked all the way back to the gate without a single rear. The crowd that had assembled at the gate to watch the rodeo show all but cheered. 'Gosh', they said, 'That's the best she's ever been!' If that's the best, I thought, I dread to think what the worst is. I bought the mare, as that's what the owner wanted. She became 'my mare'. She had plenty of other issues to address, but within a few years, became the best horse I ever owned. I had so much fun with her. As I said, she never reared again.

6. BUCKING

We have already seen how most problem behaviour is a defence mechanism that is inherent in every horse. Bucking is no different.

WHY THE HORSE BUCKS

For a wild horse, bucking is usually an attempt to throw off a predator. He isn't always successful, but it's the best he can do and always worth a try. Bucking is also used by the horse as part of the kick-back mechanism. If he can deliver a kick higher up his adversary, he can do more damage. So if your horse is bucking and kicking out, he's pretty angry.

Bucking is commonly used as a defence mechanism.

The domesticated horse uses bucking as an expression of anger. The bigger the buck, the angrier the horse. With a smaller, half buck when the horse just raises his rump, he is saying, 'I'm not happy with this.' Either the way he is asked or what he is being asked to do makes him feel pressured. He is annoyed about it and wants the rider to leave him alone. The best way for him to achieve that is to tip the rider off. What is now called 'bronco bucking' is a sign of rage and is an extremely determined effort to unseat his rider.

Most commonly, a buck seems to come out of the blue. Almost certainly, however, there have been warning signs, even if only flattened ears and some resistance to going forward. It is easy to ignore them. They don't seem to mean very much, but anger and resentment are building until they reach boiling point and the horse explodes with a buck, which can be and frequently is a violent one.

One of the most common causes of bucking is asking the horse to go into canter, or over a jump. This seems inexplicable. The horse can canter and he can jump. Why is he making such a fuss?

From the horse's point of view, we see a completely different picture. Going back to natural instinct, the horse is intrinsically lazy. All he wants is a slow, quiet, easy life. He conserves his energy for an emergency. Unlike us, he doesn't keep himself fit with lots of regular exercise. He keeps the wheels well oiled by staying slowly, but almost constantly, on the move.

If you watch a horse grazing, as long as his pasture is big enough, you will see that he is always taking the next step forward. If grass is restricted through lack of space, he moves around a lot less – which is a good reason for ensuring

adequate space, as well as grass, for your horse. The more he is allowed his natural, instinctive behaviour, the more contented he will be.

To the horse, any excessive movement is a waste of his precious energy. In his mind, galloping and jumping are only for use when danger threatens and he needs to get away fast. Thus, these energetic activities are instinctively associated with fear and danger. Asked to do them, for no good reason that he can understand, he gets annoyed about it.

This is the most important point. The bucking horse is angry. If he goes into what is now called 'bronco bucking' he is in a rage. He is screaming, 'GET OFF MY BACK!' and he means it both literally and metaphorically. He is also saying, 'Leave me alone. I don't want to do this – and I won't!'

A grazing horse is always happy to step towards the next mouthful.

We are in a bit of a double bind here. Of course there is no reason why the horse should not canter and jump. The real trouble is that he wasn't brought into it with kindness and consideration. He was either forced, or taken by surprise. Instantly, the association is formed in his mind – this is not nice and I don't like it. He starts grumbling: 'I don't like doing this, but seem to have no choice.' His grumble is a buck, a warning that he is unhappy about it.

BUCKING INTO CANTER/AFTER JUMPING

The cure for bucking depends on what the horse is being asked to do. If it is the transition into canter, the only solution is to get tough. There is no reason at all why the horse should not carry his rider along for a canter. It may use up his precious energy, but we don't really ask him to do that much. And in any case, isn't his basic nature to cooperate?

There is no choice here but to get tough to let him know in no uncertain terms that bucking into canter or after a jump is not acceptable. Unfortunately, if the horse is inclined to buck into canter, he can't be prevented from trying. It is only by dealing with it correctly that we can break him of the habit.

How to sit a buck

Look at any photo of a rodeo rider and you will see these elements. The rider leans back and raises the hand that holds the halter rope upwards. The legs are normally pushed forwards. In this position, the rodeo rider has the best chance of staying on, but of course, because rodeo horses buck so violently, they rarely do.

It is not often that our horses buck like a true rodeo horse. They are not that determined, but we, too, have the best chance of sitting out the buck and staying on if we adopt the same position. As soon as his head starts going down, take action that says, 'STOP DOING THAT!' Forget all about sitting correctly. Lean back in the saddle, brace your feet against the stirrups and yank his head up. You need to give the strongest, sharpest pull on the reins you can manage in order to give the sharpest, clearest message possible. The horse must really feel it.

The rider's position for sitting a buck.

In this position, brace your feet against the stirrups. You are then in the best possible position to sit out the antics beneath you. This is useful, not just for safety purposes, but also to make the point that the horse is not going to get you off. If he does succeed in getting you off, he learns to persevere with his tactics, which is not the lesson you want him to learn.

It is therefore imperative to get the action right; to deliver a short, sharp shock to his mouth, while staying, in both senses of the phrase, 'on top'. Getting the action right does not necessarily mean that he won't try it again, but if he does, the next buck will be less severe. He already knows he is beaten, but habit pushes him to try his luck again. He may be wrong, or just a determined optimist. Another buck might do it. He tries again, but you simply repeat the procedure.

HORSE FACT
Half the battle with problem behaviour is the confidence of knowing what to do about it. When we are confident that our response is both correct and effective, the behaviour suddenly doesn't seem so daunting. Taking these things in our stride, and if you like, pretending they're perfectly normal, sends a really positive message to the horse. He gets to thinking, 'I'm not achieving anything by this. I might as well stop doing it.' Almost inevitably, horses persevere with their resistances and evasions, either because they are in the habit of doing so, or the initial fear/resentment takes time to die down. Remember The Magic of Three! Three repetitions are usually the minimum.

As soon as the horse has stopped bucking, he should be ridden resolutely forward.

What to do next

As soon as the horse has stopped bucking, push him on to maintain the canter and then carry on as if nothing has happened. It is so tempting to then ride defensively, in anticipation of him bucking again. But you MUST take the same attitude as the horse and do what he does. After any incident, large or small, everything goes back to normal. Shortening up the reins and hanging on is riding defensively and tells the horse that you are worried. When you are worried (following the leader and doing what the others do) the horse is worried too.

The next two or three times he goes into canter, he usually tries to buck out of pure habit, but very soon his bucks become little more than a mini-buck, a gesture, until finally, he gives up altogether.

HORSE FACT

The instinct to dislodge a predator from his back has been put to good use, indeed exploited, by the rodeo horse. He has been led to believe that a rider on his back is dangerous and must be dislodged by any means possible. I might add that rodeo horses are encouraged to buck by a strap fastened tightly round the soft and sensitive area just in front of the hindquarters. It's called a kicking strap and you will always see the strap loosened off as soon as the rider has been thrown successfully.

EXPERT TIP

Ponies, in particular, are prone to bucking with young, insecure, novice riders. From the pony's point of view, the rider (who is still learning) doesn't know what they are doing, so he says, 'Please get off my back. Here we are. I'll help you!' and up goes his rump. Bingo! It works every time.

I have come across people who repeatedly put their young children back up onto a bucking pony. This is insane and no way for anyone to learn to ride, least of all a young child. As it is almost impossible (or at best extremely difficult) to persuade a horse or pony not to buck an insecure rider off, they must be found a quiet, willing, obedient pony, who will do everything that is required of a novice rider, without making any fuss. Highly trained is not necessarily the answer. All the beginner or novice needs is a quiet, steady plod who answers kindly to walk, trot and canter.

EXPERT TIP

It is no use getting someone else to 'ride the buck out of him'. As soon as you get back on, he will know the difference. In no time at all, he'll be trying to buck you off again.

SUMMARY

❖ Bucking is a sure sign of anger. The bigger the buck, the more angry the horse.
❖ Bronco bucking is a scream of rage.
❖ All the horse wants is a slow, quiet, easy life. Using his precious energy goes against the grain.
❖ To confront bucking into canter/jumping – you must get tough:
  – Lean back
  – Brace your feet against the stirrups
  – Yank the horse's head up forcefully
After the incident, carry on as if nothing has happened.

BUCKING 'OUT OF THE BLUE'

This is another proposition altogether, and seemingly happens out of nowhere. It often occurs when working in a school or arena, but can happen anywhere at any time.

Why is the horse angry? More often than not, it is the way he is ridden, but it can also be what he is asked to do. As we have found out, it goes against the grain for him to do lots of fast work in trot and/or canter, and to go endlessly round a small, enclosed space is equally tiresome. What's more, being held constantly in an uncomfortable position makes his neck and back muscles ache. All these things can make him angry and resentful. Blithely, we carry on.

Meanwhile, the horse is asking himself, 'Why am I putting up with this?' until he can't take it any more. Then he explodes, often into what we call 'bronco bucking'. It is too frequently not understood that it takes a long time of carefully building up the correct muscles for the horse to carry himself for an extended period of time in what is often called 'the correct outline'. No horse normally carries himself this way for more than a few seconds at a time. To do it on demand, he must be properly prepared and trained. Proper preparation and training *do not* involve the use of inappropriate bits, gadgets, or coercive techniques, which will simply add to the horse's discomfort and distress.

WHAT I WOULD DO

The initial response

With such a horse, I would take him right back to basics, to show him that working in a school or arena (which is alien and uncomfortable for him) is not so bad after all. I have a clear set of achievable targets. The first is a calm, quiet walk.

A calm, quiet walk is the first step in showing a horse that schooling is not so bad.

All I want at this stage is that he goes where I ask him to go in a quiet, submissive manner. I am asking for his willing cooperation at the most basic level of obedience. This is achieved by ambling randomly around the arena on a long, loose rein, giving the horse the freedom to carry himself as he chooses. From here, I want him to relax into his natural way of going, which is slow and easy. If the horse isn't used to this freedom, it may take a while, but I will persevere. I know that, in his heart, this is what he likes the best.

To help him relax, I change the rein frequently, across the short and long sides and across all the diagonals. I put him round a combination of circles large and small and any other figures that come to mind. It doesn't matter where he is asked to go, as long as it is constantly changing. This gets his attention focused on me, along with the understanding that doing what I ask isn't so hard after all. The first two or three sessions may well be focused mostly on getting him to relax.

Along the way, I will be constantly body checking. I want my body language, or the message I am sending, to be spot on. I also want my inner stillness to shine through. This horse is tense and anxious. He needs all the help he can get.

In this frame, he has nothing at all to get angry about. At the same time, he is learning (or re-learning) how to be light and responsive. He becomes submissive and easy in himself, not only willing but able to cooperate.

The second achievable target

When he is quiet, responsive and obedient in walk (and not before) I set the second achievable target, which is to do the same in trot. Still on a long, loose rein, I squeeze him gently into trot. At first, I don't ask for much. Half a long side may be enough, if he seems anxious about it. Basically, I accept as much as he is willing to give. All I want here is to establish the principle – that he trots when asked and goes along calmly and quietly.

Once the horse is calm and responsive in walk, proceed to an undemanding trot.

As we progress and can trot for longer, I stick to the same routine, incorporating plenty of rein changes, circles, figures and so on. Again, the principle here is basic obedience to the simple aids and the essence is to keep it all very slow, quiet and easy.

If he is a little speedy on first being asked to trot, I will either let him go on, find out for himself that there is no need for it and slow down by himself, or I will gently restrain him and 'suggest' he slows down. It depends on the horse.

The third achievable target

Once again, the horse discovers that cooperation is easy. He can do this too. Finally, when trot is quiet, easy and responsive, I move carefully into canter, starting on a long straight side on the outside track, to make it easy for him. By now, we are settling into an easy, trusting relationship. He has settled into this easy way of going, so canter is not normally a problem. He canters on beautifully for some little way. How lovely! Having made the point, I give him his due reward and return quietly to trot and walk – if he hasn't already slowed down by himself.

When all of this is satisfactory and done without any fuss, the horse is ready to go on (if required) to the higher discipline of working on a contact – but not before. And even then, it must be approached with caution. We know he can be explosive, so periods of disciplined work must be kept short and followed by the rest and relaxation of ambling about on a long, loose rein. Think of it as a tea/coffee-break. No worker in this country thinks they can survive without them, but in any event, they do break up what can otherwise be a stressful, tedious or boring day.

NB: *It is always advisable to give 'tea-breaks' during schooling, because it is quite hard and stressful for the horse.*

Hacking

Another option, and one that I would incorporate, is to go hacking, again on a loose, easy rein. Of all the riding we do, hacking is the most relaxing for the horse – as long as we allow him to be easy and relaxed that is. If we hack out in 'work mode', on rein/leg contact and in the 'correct outline', he is fully justified in getting angry and throwing in a few bucks.

SUMMARY

❖ Going endlessly round a small, enclosed space and/or doing lots of fast work are inclined to make the horse angry/resentful.

❖ Working in what is perceived to be the 'correct outline' is extremely difficult, unless he has been properly prepared.

❖ He explodes when he can't take any more.

❖ He needs to find out that working in an arena isn't so bad after all.

❖ This is done by going right back to basics.

❖ Use achievable targets to progress the horse.

❖ When schooling, give 'tea-breaks' along the way.

BUCKING ON RETURNING TO WORK

The final cause of bucking (and other difficulties) is a long period of rest, as a consequence of injury, ill-health, or for any other reason. The horse comes to believe that his riding days are over. No more work! Bearing in mind his ancestry and the perfect life, a horse off work adapts very easily to his new regime. If it goes on for long enough, such as a few weeks or months, the horse, if he could talk, might say: 'Fantastic. That's the end of my riding career. I'm free at last!'

From the horse's point of view, imagine his shock and horror when, one fine day, he is brought from his place of rest and ridden. He couldn't have been more wrong. This was only a temporary respite, not a permanent state of affairs. Oh yes, he's angry and resentful. Before long, he turns into a bucking bronco with other, related difficulties. He won't be tacked up, or mounted. He fidgets while he's groomed and may also decide not to let himself be caught in the first place. Anything to get out of this awful turn of events.

The moral of this story is to bring him back into work slowly and gently. The concept of achievable targets is also useful here, although more along the lines of 'How much is he willing to do?'

WHAT I WOULD DO

I would keep it all very easy at first, mostly in walk and not for long. He needs to get used to the idea again. Slowly, I would build up the speed and the workload, as he finds it acceptable. A little trotting, but not for long, then go back into walk … and so on, until slowly, I would bring him back to where he was before his holiday.

In other words, the assumption must NOT be made that you can pick him up where you left off and he will be the same as before. He isn't. He's had too long a holiday.

SUMMARY

❖ A long period of rest leads the horse to believe that he no longer has to work.

❖ He is shocked and to find that his life as a riding horse is not over after all.

❖ Bristling with anger and resentment, he shows it by bucking – and other difficulties.

❖ He needs to be brought back into work very slowly and gently, keeping his work easy and comfortable.

7. SPOOKING

As we know, horses are suspicious of unfamiliar objects, be they large or small. This is normal and natural for the wild horse. They know their territory so well, that if they haven't seen it before, it might be dangerous.

WHY HORSES SPOOK

Spooking is a defence mechanism. Horses' immediate, instinctive reaction is to give an unfamiliar object their full attention and, if necessary, take evasive action, poised to run. They skirt round it, make a detour and often go into trot, in preparation for a speedy getaway. If it doesn't move and/or shows no sign of a threat, they relax and resume their grazing or migrating – whatever they were doing before.

If they see the same object again, in the same place, they are less wary, but still cautious and may take evasive action – just in case. By the third time, if there is a third time, they barely take any notice. They just keep a wary eye on it, to make sure they haven't misjudged. The Magic of Three again!

A horse confronted by an unusual object may stop dead.

If the same object turns up in a different place, or is encountered from a different direction, it is seen as completely new and different and they go through the same procedure all over again. Only when this same object keeps popping up all over the place do they finally get used to it and take it for what it is … a harmless object.

As we subject our horses to situations not normally experienced by wild horses, they have a wider range of reactions. Some may stop dead and refuse to go forward. They stand as if transfixed by fear and stare at it, almost willing it to jump out and bite them. (That would make them move!) Each reaction must be taken on its own merits and treated accordingly.

WHAT I WOULD DO

My first response is to stop and wait, sit still and do nothing. The horse is assessing the situation and also waiting to find out what I'm going to do. If I push on forcefully, that will be his cue to either plant his feet more firmly or, worse still, back away.

I wait until he seems bored with standing there and then politely ask him to go on. I may get just one or two hesitant steps but that's OK. We are headed in the right direction. And so I repeat the procedure until we are safely past.

Other horses don't stop and wait, but run away as fast as possible in any direction – the headless chicken syndrome. Most, however, do what horses normally do when they see a suspicious object for the first time – they take evasive action, watching carefully, as they go by.

In a situation such as that in the adjacent photos, I let the horse take responsibility for himself and do nothing. This is what his instinct tells him to do and it is not my place to interfere. He needs this reaction, so I allow him to have it. Only in this way can he satisfy himself that there is nothing to fear. Once past the object, we carry on as if nothing has happened.

Another reaction to seeing a suspicious object, is to take evasive action.

Where things go wrong is when the rider tries to take control. Now the horse is really scared. He knows how to protect himself, but is not allowed to; his rider has other ideas.

Over-controlling

Another common cause of spooking is riding in too controlled a way. Too much pressure on the reins makes the horse nervous, even more so if he is never allowed to look at anything. This applies particularly to hacking out, but can also apply to schooling. In a general state of nervousness, he looks for actual things to be frightened about. This is called a 'displacement activity', which can be provoked by something he sees every day, such as jump stands at the side of the arena. It is not that he is actually frightened of the object, but that he needs to express his nervousness.

The nervous rider

Likewise, nervousness in the rider is transmitted to the horse. He becomes nervous too and, again, looks for a displacement activity. Indeed, a symptom of the nervous rider is hanging onto the reins for security – which brings us back to over-controlling.

From the horse's point of view, his first thought in such circumstances is, 'Here's something I'm not sure about', but he usually wouldn't think too much of it, unless something else happens. What tends to happen is that 'the boss upstairs' tries to take control. Now the horse gets confused. His instincts are telling him what to do, but his rider is trying to make him do something else.

He may get a bit frantic and head towards panic. His attention now turns away from 'the thing' and to the controlling. Suddenly, his mouth is very uncomfortable. He doesn't like it. Additionally, he makes a connection: 'I see an object I'm worried about and I am controlled from above'. Now he is confused and the horse who spooks or shies at everything is born.

This is not *always* how spooking develops, but it does generally apply to horses who have not had a well-rounded basic education and therefore have a propensity for it. Spookiness seems to come out of the blue, usually soon after the purchase of a new horse. He has been tried and tested and shown no sign of spooking. He is brought to his new home and, before long, he is spooking at all sorts of things – blades of grass included.

New home syndrome

The underlying principle just mentioned is essentially the same with 'New Home Syndrome'. The horse was perfectly happy in and well adjusted to the home he came from. Everything about his life was comfortable and familiar. In his new home, everything has changed and horses don't like change at the best of times. On top of everything else, he may feel over-controlled.

The horse is in a quandary. He can't do what all his instincts are telling him to do. He must do as he's told, but this is not the spirit of cooperation he's looking for. He does his best for so long, usually a week or two. Then the cracks start to show. He is not a happy horse. His new life makes him nervous.

He may be allowed his natural reaction, but has the impression that the rider is scared by it. It's all very subtle, but the horse is so sensitive that he is capable of picking up the slightest shadow of doubt or fear. As we have found out, if his rider is worried, he is too. Again, this would be a horse who lacks the confidence derived from the right start in life. The horse who has reached full emotional maturity and is completely self-assured is not too bothered by a little rider insecurity. He has enough confidence for both.

DEALING WITH SPOOKING

Basic responses

As we will see, there may be different root causes of spooking, but whatever the apparent cause, I have only one rule in this situation and that is to allow the horse his own, natural, reaction – whatever that may be. If he wants to stop, drop his nose and inspect the object, I allow it. I sit very quietly and wait for him to satisfy his curiosity. I know when he's satisfied, because he loses interest and looks away. When this happens, I know he's ready to go on.

If it seems necessary, I dismount to act as leader and show by example. I remain calm, centred and grounded and wait for him to show me that the moment has passed. I will remount shortly afterwards and carry on as if nothing has happened.

He may want to make a detour, while looking at it. That is fine: no problem here at all. I allow him to make a detour. (The only time this can be a problem is on a busy road. Unfortunately, all we can do here is put our faith in circumstance and any approaching drivers. It is far more important to allow the horse to do what he needs to do than attempt to 'keep him under control'. This is when accidents happen, as the horse panics and does something infinitely worse, like jump wildly into the path of an oncoming vehicle. Left to his own devices, without the misguided coercion, no horse would ever do that.)

NB: If your horse has a problem with spooking badly, then either stay away from busy roads, or dismount and lead in hand.

Another reaction a horse may have is to make a small detour and speed up a little, as if to run away from the object. This too, I allow, knowing full well that he will slow down of his own accord soon enough, as long as I leave him to get on with it and don't interfere.

Alternatively, he may startle forward at a faster gait and with his head in the air, in which case, I give him a chance to sort himself out.

If necessary, it can be helpful to dismount and offer reassurance while the horse inspects the object.

In such a situation, you should simply sit still and do absolutely nothing. Remind yourself firmly of the wild horse who only runs a short distance, unless he is chased. As long as the object doesn't come after him (which of course, normally, it doesn't) he will soon slow down of his own accord and carry on as he was before.

It also pays to bear in mind that horses run forward on a straight line. They do not zigzag or dodge, like a rabbit. This means you can sit out their spooky little run, without fear of falling off.

If the horse wants to speed up away from the object, allow him to do so.

However, you need to know what to do if, for any reason, the horse doesn't slow down as quickly as you had expected. You are sitting there quietly but can *feel* the surge continuing. Above all, don't panic. Tune in to the feeling. You will know within a few strides. At this point, do a quick body check, your legs in particular. They must not be gripping and urging him forward. Then pick (shorten) your reins and start applying 'give and take'. Remember that the horse is scared so you don't want to frighten him any more by hauling on the reins.

Very nervous horses

If the horse is *very* nervous or fearful of something, I will dismount and lead. As soon as I get off his back, he has one less thing to worry about. I can also exert more influence from the ground, showing by example, as well as demonstrating my qualities of leadership.

NB: In this situation, always endeavour to put yourself between the horse and the object. If he is going to jump anywhere, it will be sideways, away from it.

Steady improvement

By giving in to the horse and allowing his natural reactions, slowly but surely he stops finding things to spook at. Most commonly, the very thing that was making him nervous was the controlling. More often than not, he wasn't really scared of the object. The spooking was his way of telling us that something was wrong. Now he has nothing to be nervous about.

Habitual spooking

When dealing with long-term habitual spooking, another problem arises. Natural reactions in themselves become a habit. Fear is no longer at the root of this behaviour. This is OK on one level: we have shown that we understand his fears and given him the opportunity to sort himself out. When it becomes evident and I am *fully convinced* that this behaviour is now just a game, I change tactic completely. No longer is he allowed to do his own thing. From now on, he is told what to do.

NB: *It is better to wait too long to make this decision, than rush into it too soon. You must be fully convinced that now he is just having you on. The indicator is that there has been no real progress shown.*

I would now start riding in a very controlled way, keeping a reasonable rein contact (although not too demanding or restrictive) and riding him firmly forward. From this point on, he is not allowed to look at anything.

Don't try to run before you can walk!

The first achievable target is to walk forwards on the straight line. It may be several rides before he understands and accepts that his previous behaviour is no longer tolerated. At first, he doesn't walk nicely. He is anxious and fidgety, trying to get back to the familiar, comfortable place he was in before. He may snatch at the bit and try throwing his head around but, on such a horse, I remain calm and above all constant. Body checking as I go, I keep it firmly lodged in my mind that I want him to be calm and constant too.

Mind over matter

Curiously perhaps, if we keep the immediate goal, or achievable target, fixed firmly in the mind, we find that when we are soft and receptive, what we need to do comes by itself. It must be the immediate goal though. If we set cantering along a glorious beach as the goal, this comes into the category of 'end-gaming'. The immediate goal here is a calm and consistent walk.

Expectations

Progress in this kind of retraining is likely to be slow. First, we get moments. Oh wow! This is going well. He's got it. Then he slips back, as if to say, 'Fooled you!' But he is not trying to fool us. He's not that clever. He is simply finding it difficult to accept a new way of going. So we are not disheartened. On the contrary, this is a good sign. It means the message is getting through.

The moments become more frequent, or longer, until eventually, they all merge together. The horse gives up and submits. Now, we can think about the next achievable target, which is the same consistent behaviour in trot.

In trot, we carry on as before, not allowing him to look at anything and keeping his mind fixed firmly on the job. By now, he is getting the idea. Spooking and anything connected to it is now off the agenda. Normally, he moves on into trot without any difficulty. This way of going has become the norm.

When walk and trot are exactly as we want them, we can start to relax. There is no further need to ride firmly forward. He has forgotten about spooking. It is not an issue any more. Should there ever be a slight relapse, we revert to tighter control. Above all, we do not worry about it.

How long does it take?
Probably several weeks is the short answer, although much depends on how often he is ridden and what he may or may not do in between. Broadly, the longer any habit has been established, the longer it will take him to get over it – spooking included.

SUMMARY
❖ The spooky horse is nervous.
❖ Over-controlling and/or a nervous rider make the horse nervous.
❖ The nervous horse finds a displacement activity.
❖ Nervousness commonly starts when the horse moves to a new home.
❖ He must be allowed his natural reaction. It is his decision, not ours.
  Natural reactions include:
  – Stopping to inspect the object of suspicion.
  – Making a detour.
  – Making a detour and speeding up.
  – Simply running away.
  If allowing natural reaction becomes a habit, change the tactic
  and take control.

8. BOLTING

When the riding horse bolts for the first time, he is doing what wild horses do, which is to run away, as fast as possible. When they feel it is safe to do so, they slow down, stop running and everything goes back to normal.

We see this clearly when, loose in his field, a horse is suddenly spooked or startled. He runs so far then slows down of his own accord. This is assuming that there is no further provocation. Unfortunately for him, when ridden, there usually is. The provocation is the rider, who is usually terrified and hauling away at his mouth.

Bolting horses run as fast as they can, until they feel it is safe to slow down.

WHY HORSES BOLT

Instinctively, horses move away from pressure. If the pressure is too much, they run away from it. The mouth being so sensitive, excessive pressure on the bit can easily provoke them into running away. In so doing, they make their situation worse.

Most commonly, it is a sudden spook or startle that escalates into a mad, panic bolt. The rider grabs at the reins and starts pulling. Away goes the horse, not running now away from the original startle, but from the panic reaction on top. Action and reaction are at work again. Canter speeds up into a manic gallop; he's attempting to run away from the pressure on the bit.

From the horse's point of view, he has only one thought: 'Get me out of here – fast!' He goes into panic. He wants to get rid of the pressure in his mouth. The best he can do is run away from it. Somehow or other, the rider deals with it, but then becomes so anxious that the horse may bolt again, that he is held in on a short, tight rein. This is precisely what the horse was running away from. Now, he too is nervous and will bolt again on the slightest pretext. The pressure keeps on coming; it doesn't go away, which is how constant, unrelenting pressure on the reins becomes a 'go-faster' signal and why we must always use the reins with the utmost discretion and sensitivity.

The confirmed bolter is, however, beyond sensitivity. He is consumed by fear. His only hope, according to his book of rules, is to keep running, as far and fast as possible. Eventually, he slows down, either out of sheer exhaustion, or because the rider's demands finally get through to him. When the same situation recurs, off he goes again and the habit is quickly established.

DEALING WITH BOLTING

General principles

The essence is to get on top of the situation, by the use of aids that cut through the panic. On a horse showing signs of bolting, as he surges forward, I do a quick body check, or more precisely, I check what my legs are doing. The last thing I want to do is urge him on even more. Confident that my legs are not urging him forward, I go straight into 'give and take' mode.

NB: It may sound as if the preparation takes a long time, but in reality, we are talking about seconds. It also takes a second or two for a horse to gather up speed, which is long enough for a body check and rein adjustment.

To let him know that running away is not an option, I shorten up my reins and take a strong pull for the duration of two strides. I then loosen the rein and release the pressure for another two strides. In this way, I create a rhythm. Effectively, the pull says 'Slow down'. The release says 'Please'. However, the pull must be strong enough to cut through the fear and be 'heard'. If it's not strong enough, he won't take any notice. If I need to, I will lean back on the pull, to put my bodyweight behind it. If necessary, I make the pull sharp as well as strong and jag at his mouth. This is a signal that must be felt, so the release must be equally clear.

Within a few strides, I notice that the horse is listening. He is starting to respond, so I reduce the strength of pull a little. The pull/release rhythm stays the same, fitting it into his strides. As he starts to slow down, the rhythm changes. I change with it.

If a spook or startle has escalated into a bolt, I want to reinforce his natural instincts and help him pull up. I maintain the pull/release rhythm until the panic has subsided and he's cantering normally. He now feels in safe hands, so it doesn't take long. I can pull him up normally and carry on as if nothing has happened.

Bolting away from canter

Usually, it is an over-active, speedy kind of horse (what is sometimes called 'forward-going') who habitually bolts away from canter. With such a horse, I prepare in advance. Before asking for canter, I surreptitiously extend my arms and slide my hands down the reins to make them shorter. I do it sneakily, because I don't want to give him any warning or provocation – as I demonstrate in the accompanying photos.

1. I start with my hands in the normal position, elbows tucked into my sides and reins with a comfortable contact, not pulling or restraining the horse in any way.

2. Preparing to canter, I start my hands creeping down the reins. As you can see, I begin to reach forward by lightly opening my fingers and moving my hands further down. As my arms are extended, my body position stays the same.

3. With my body still upright and having reached forward as far as I can, my fingers are closed into a normal hold and I am ready now to use the reins effectively.

Adjusting the reins quietly, prior to cantering.

Knowing that he is poised to bolt, the aid to canter is barely perceptible, more a tightening of the calf muscles than an actual squeeze. As he gathers himself up to surge forward, I cut in with the first strong pull. At the same time, I check that my legs are in the right place. Then I enter into the pull/release rhythm. Within a few strides, he is cantering at a reasonable speed. I maintain it by maintaining the pull/release rhythm.

It is also important to maintain an upright position. Fear tends to make us crouch, or curl up into a foetal position. In leaning forward/crouching, we transmit our fear to the horse, which is not good for the horse. He has enough fear of his own. He doesn't need ours. What he needs from us is a clear head and the confidence to take control, not of him, but of the situation.

With a long-term, confirmed bolter and/or older horse there is not likely to be total resolution. We may always have to ride canter in this way. Where the problem has only developed recently in a younger horse, he does learn in the end that there is no need to run away from canter and all is well.

HORSE FACT
Not for nothing is panic called 'blind'. When panic sets in, horses (like us) stop thinking clearly, which can lead them into doing things they wouldn't normally do, like scramble through barbed wire or collide with trucks. It is imperative therefore, that we get our signals right, so as to minimise the panic.

HORSE FACT
It is from here we get the phrase 'dead in the mouth'. Heavy hands and too much pulling on the reins cause the horse to become desensitised to them. He simply switches off. Equally, he can become 'dead to the leg' for the same reason. Too much kicking, or battering his ribs and he learns to ignore it completely.

An alternative method

A useful ploy is to keep running the horse up a long, steep hill. This, of course does depend on the presence of long, steep hills in the locality. But if you are so lucky, there is no better way of showing the horse that he has no need to expend so much energy. Point him at the hill, put him into canter, give away the reins and leave him to work it out by himself. And the less fit he is, the better. The crucial point here is to give away the reins. Let them go really loose, so there is no contact with the mouth at all. In this way, the horse teaches himself the lesson. He is free to go as fast as he likes, but galloping up a steep hill is really hard work. He decides for himself that it's not worth the effort and slows down.

Do this two or three times, then ask him to canter on the flat. If he has learned the lesson, he canters along nicely without any interference from you. If he hasn't learned the lesson, this may not be the way to go, but it is always worth a try.

FROM MY CASE BOOK

We called him 'Dylan the Charger': he was a 13.2hh Hackney cross, eight years old and a confirmed bolter. Everything about him was speedy. Under saddle, he didn't know the meaning of the words 'slow' or 'relaxed'. It actually took a few years to persuade him that he didn't have to be trying to run away all the time.

To start with, I had to put him in a really strong bit. He couldn't 'hear' it otherwise. I put him in a plain curb, with the longest shanks I could find. If he didn't feel this bit, he wouldn't feel anything and he *had* to know that he could be stopped. From then on, it was a case of constantly giving away and re-taking the reins in every gait. Gradually, the spaces between re-taking the reins became longer until the magic moment came when he managed a proper canter on a completely loose rein and stopped very nicely at the end of it.

We weren't yet quite at the end of it but Dylan had certainly got the idea. It was time to his downgrade his bit to a Kimblewick. Although he was fairly good by then, he still had moments when we needed a little more control. For a while, he was put into a hackamore to take all pressure off his mouth. Then an amazing thing happened. A girl called Lou came into his life.

One day, she asked if she could ride him. I was doubtful. From what I had seen of her riding, she was a little nervous. That wouldn't do Dylan any good at all. I said she could ride him up the field, as long as she was led. This was bareback in a halter. She was happy with that.

A little while later, she asked if she could ride him out on her own. I wasn't at all sure about that, but said she could, as long as she promised to dismount and lead if the going got tough. She came back glowing. Dylan had been absolutely fine – even in canter.

Before I knew it, she was riding him out bareback in a halter, walk, trot and canter and having a wonderful time.

I am pleased to tell you that Lou bought Dylan. We saw them a few years later. Dylan looked so well, fit and happy and Lou was as pleased as punch. I presume they lived happily ever after.

SUMMARY

❖ Constant, unrelenting pressure on the bit becomes a 'go faster' signal.
❖ Gripping legs make the situation worse.
❖ The horse slows down of his own accord when the need for action has been met and the fear subsided.
❖ The confirmed bolter is beyond sensitivity and needs rider intervention. This takes the form of a rhythmic 'give and take' on the reins:
  – A pull on the reins says 'slow down'; the release says 'please'.
  – Leaning back and using bodyweight reinforces the pull.
❖ Prevent a bolt by being prepared and on top of the situation.
❖ Running him up a steep hill may persuade the horse to stop bolting.

9. GOING BACKWARDS

Wild horses rarely have occasion to go backwards but, if they do, they will only go as far as is absolutely necessary. Their rear-view vision is not so good and their feet are precious. They prefer to see where they are putting them. Neither do they like falling down ditches or bumping into things, either of which can happen when a horse goes into reverse. Backing away from anything is a last resort, and stops at the earliest opportunity. This inclination can be used to our advantage.

Try it yourself and see what it feels like. Notice how your legs don't seem to work very well and how hard it is to see where you're going. We are not really designed to go backwards – and neither is the horse.

UNDER SADDLE

From the horse's point of view, (unless he has been trained in rein-back and understands that this is what is required) going backwards always happens when the rider is trying to make the horse go forwards. He plants his feet and refuses to move. The rider goes into autopilot and kicks harder. The horse says, 'Absolutely not! I cannot and will not go forwards'. The rider kicks harder still, but the kicking is all too much. The horse doesn't like it and feels he must do what he can to get away. He goes into reverse.

Frustrated and annoyed, the rider keeps on kicking. In response, the horse continues on his backward path, disliking every second, but now feeling that he has no choice. This is when the horse falls into a ditch, or collides with an immovable object. Everyone is brought abruptly to their senses.

Dealing with going backwards under saddle

Actually, it couldn't be easier. As soon as a horse starts going backwards, I will sit with complete inner stillness and do absolutely nothing. I leave the reins loose, leaving the way open, if you like, for the horse to go forwards. My feet sit quietly on the stirrups, doing nothing. Sitting there, watching the world go by, I wait for the horse to stop by himself. Without any interference from me, this is likely to happen sooner rather than later.

I also check to see if he is backing towards a solid object, such as a hedge, fence, wall or gate. I know that if he gets that far, bumping into it will bring his backward path to an abrupt halt – so I don't worry about it. It has never happened so far, but if he were backing towards danger, such as a ditch or road, I would jump off before he got there.

When he stops, which he does eventually, I stop and wait, sit still and do nothing. Meanwhile, I watch the horse's head. He may have stopped going backwards, but he is still, momentarily, in a rebellious state of mind. His head is up and ears back.

Finding that there are no signals from above, a curious thing happens. He

Stillness and patience in the rider pay dividends in solving the problem of gong backwards.

loses interest, forgets about his rebellion and starts looking around. Reading the signs, I know that this is the moment to squeeze him forward – which I do normally, as if nothing has happened.

Going into reverse hasn't achieved anything. His rider has just accepted his little tantrum. He thinks no more of it and that's the end of it. Additionally, he now has trust in the leadership qualities of his rider.

What happens next?

What sometimes happens is that he gets back to the point of the original resistance and stops, as if there is a line on the ground and he is unable to cross it. Commonly, this point, or line, is the edge of his comfort zone. I don't want to reinforce the backward response, so I have to do something else. He is unable to go any further because he lacks the confidence and feels insecure. In this case, I simply dismount and lead him through his block.

I take the reins over his head and use them like a pair of lead-ropes. I then walk forwards to show by example and put myself in the position of leader. The horse is now in the more comfortable position of follower.

Where he is still resistant to following me, I use the principle of 'equal and opposite reaction'. I maintain a tension on the reins, which is equal to the resistance. This lets the horse know that I am not giving in, but I am also not fighting over it. If he stops, I stop too, but maintain the tension, until the moment is right to give a little tug. In this way, I establish a dialogue. It goes something like this:

Horse: 'I'm nervous about this. I don't want to go.'
Me: 'I know, but really it isn't as bad as you think it is.'
Horse: 'Yes it is. I know it is. I went there yesterday.'
Me: 'Oh, come on. You're just being a big baby. Stop messing about.'
Horse: 'Oh, all right then. If you insist!'

In this way, I show him that I am listening, respecting his opinion, but at the same time, informing him of what I want and asking for his cooperation. When the horse has accepted his fate and is going along willingly, I mount, or remount and continue.

Overcoming mental blocks may take some time. Equally, we may overcome one block, only to find another a few minutes later. In which case, we simply repeat the procedure until the horse is satisfied that there is nothing to fear. However, each time the procedure is repeated, it should get easier. If not, either we are not doing it correctly, or something else is wrong, which needs to be addressed.

FROM MY CASE BOOK

Pudsie was a character, a 13.2hh Arab cross and a nervous little girl. Among other idiosyncrasies, she would go into reverse at the drop of a hat. I have never known a horse or pony so willing and able to reverse so far, or so fast. Had there been competitions for going backwards, she would have won them all.

When it happened, there was no choice but to wave goodbye to my companions and let her get on with it. Sometimes she bumped into a hedge or fence and that got her going again. Other times, I just sat it out. Happily, once she'd had her little resistance and made her point, she would keep going afterwards. In any case, we usually had some catching up to do, as anyone else was way ahead. She also hated getting left behind, so that was useful.

The last time she did it, we were on a small country lane. My daughter was riding her. Seemingly out of the blue, she stopped and went into reverse. I stopped the horse I was riding to watch. Pudsie went off with such determination I honestly thought she was going to back up all the way home. Or perhaps not! Home was about a mile away.

They disappeared round a bend. I sat and waited. Before too long, they reappeared, trotting along nicely. We continued our ride and Pudsie never backed up again.

ON THE GROUND

Horses may also go backwards when we are on the ground and trying to pull them forwards. The reason is the same. They don't want to go, although it may have nothing to do with their comfort zone. Usually, it is because they don't like what's ahead of them, either an activity (riding) or separation from their friends and companions. Or it may be something more tangible, like loading into a lorry or trailer.

Whatever the reason, once again, we use the same approach. If the horse starts going backwards, we let him carry on until he stops by himself. We then assess the situation and decide what to do next. The principle of 'equal and opposite reaction' (which is similar to 'give and take' on the reins) may do the trick. If not, we must look deeper and address the underlying reason, which will be considered later (see Chapter 16).

SUMMARY

❖ Horses dislike going backwards. Their rear-view vision isn't so good.
❖ Urging forward/kicking on makes the situation worse.
❖ Sit still and do nothing.
❖ Allow the horse to stop of his own accord.
❖ Backing into a (safe) solid object is also helpful.
❖ After backing up, the horse is usually willing to go forward normally.
❖ Dismounting and leading forward is the only other option.
❖ Overcoming a mental block may take some time.

10. REFUSING TO GO FORWARDS

The horse goes so far, then won't go any further. He will go backwards (see previous chapter), sideways or round in a circle. He will grow roots from his feet and refuse to move at all, but go forwards – never! What is going on in his head?

If a wild horse ever has any reason to doubt the wisdom or safety of going forwards, he stops and looks around, to see what anyone else is doing. (Stick together; do what the others do.) Generally, he will take his cue from the majority. The horse is so finely tuned to possible danger that he rarely acts alone.

From the horse's point of view, whether ridden or leading, the horse who refuses to go forwards is literally voting with his feet. It's a vote of no confidence – but about what? There are several possibilities. Each situation must be analysed and treated accordingly. When we know *why* he is stopping and refusing to go forwards, we have a better idea of what to do about it. (For example, refusing to go forwards can be a precursor to, or associated with the reasons for, rearing – see Chapter 5.)

LACK OF CONFIDENCE

The horse hasn't been there before and lacks confidence. He must be introduced slowly and carefully and without putting any pressure on him.

WHAT I WOULD DO

If the horse is new to the area, I might start by leading him out in hand, as if going out for a walk together. This would be to introduce him to the surroundings, without the burden of a rider. My objective would be to amble along comfortably, but he would doubtless want to stop and look at things. I would let him do this, but not for long. I want him to know that I make the decisions, so after a little look, I would ask him to walk on again.

If we reach a point of real resistance, a moment when he says, 'I really can't go any further' I assess the situation. If I think he's had as much as he can take for one day, I persuade him to go a tiny bit further by using the 'give and take on the rope' technique. I want him know that I make the decisions, but as soon as he's complied, I give in to him, turn him round and take him home.

Ideally, I choose a circular route that brings us naturally and easily back on the homeward track. I start with a small one and gradually increase the distance. After two, three, or maybe four outings, I go back to the first, small circuit and ride him round it. By now, he is beginning to know both me, and the area, so this generally comes easily enough. Then I start to get the measure of him as a riding horse.

On principle, I give him a loose, free rein and allow him to carry himself as he chooses. However, if he has only ever been ridden on a contact, I keep the reins shorter than I normally would. Basically, I want to give him the

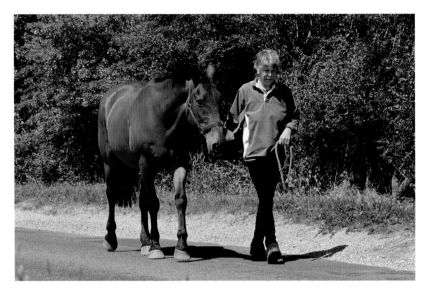

Leading out in hand can be a confidence-booster for a horse in a new area.

freedom to be himself and to be comfortable and relaxed with me. Only then can he go freely forwards.

Don't try to run before you can walk!
I also tend to do early rides mostly in walk. If he's going to play up in any way, it will be easier to deal with in walk. Additionally, I want to make the experience of riding easy and undemanding, so I will only go into trot when I feel the horse is ready. In trot, I accept only as much as he is willing to give. If he wants to trot on a bit and is behaving well, I allow it. If he doesn't seem too keen, I don't ask for much. This is a confidence-building exercise. As his confidence increases, he will give more.

PREVIOUS BAD EXPERIENCE

The horse has been there before, but knows that he's going to get a hard time and doesn't want to repeat the experience.

This mostly happens when we ask for too much, or more than he is willing to give. This can be in the context of both schooling and hacking out. We expect a lot of the horse, but he isn't always ready.

WHAT I WOULD DO (SCHOOLING)

The principle here is to make it easy for the horse. With schooling, I would go back a few steps. If necessary, I would go right back to basics, working on a loose, free rein and allowing the horse to carry himself as he chooses (see Chapter 6). The essence here is for him to find out that this isn't so hard or unpleasant after all and he has no reason to refuse to go forwards.

Slowly, I would work my way back to where he was before, *but* I would also give him breaks along the way by going back to ambling about on a loose, free rein. You can tell when the horse needs a break, because he starts to get a wee bit difficult. However, better by far is to give him a break *before* he starts voicing objections. When he has just done exceptionally well is a good time for a few minutes of rest and relaxation.

WHAT I WOULD DO (HACKING)
Refusing to go hacking is a slightly different kettle of fish. First, I ask myself a few questions. Am I asking anything of him which he finds difficult or unpleasant? Am I expecting him to go places he's not happy about? Am I overfacing him and trying to take him too far? Am I nagging at him in any way? This includes things like nagging at him to maintain a faster speed than is comfortable for him. Am I nagging at his mouth?

The next question is the important one. How can I make it easy for him? In the first place, I might have to start the ride by leading him from the ground. This is to give the idea that we are going out, whether he likes it or not. Only when he is settled and coming along willingly enough, would I mount and start riding. Then I would address any of the issues that I thought might be the cause of his resistance.

RIDER ISSUES

Rider holding him in/hanging on to his head
Essentially, the horse who refuses to go forwards in this situation is doing what he is being asked to do. In simple terms, pressure on the bit means slow down or stop. If he's not too keen anyway, this is the perfect excuse. Too much kicking can also cause the horse to fight back by refusing to do anything (see Chapter 9).

WHAT I WOULD DO
With a horse who has been ridden in a such a way as to induce this mindset, I would simply release the reins and open the way for him to go forwards. I would then use my legs normally to squeeze him forward. If his only problem is that the reins are too short/tight, releasing the reins will resolve it immediately.

Rider is insecure and/or nervous
This rider should be put on the leading-rein or safely behind a reliable lead horse, until they have gained the necessary skills and confidence. Only time and good experience can put these into place. If the rider has to struggle, building confidence is impossible. It may also be that the rider has the wrong horse and should find another one.

The riding style doesn't suit the horse

As we have discovered, horses get used to a particular style of riding. If it changes, they can feel lost and insecure, resulting in a lack of desire to do anything.

WHAT I WOULD DO

On such a horse, I would play around with rein and leg contact and find out what suits him best. Ideally, I would move the horse towards accepting a loose rein and the simple aids, at least for general purposes, such as hacking.

Horse knows he can get away with it

This horse has been spoilt: he is used to getting his own way. As soon as a rider gets on, he switches off.

WHAT I WOULD DO

First, I would try repeatedly squeezing (not kicking) at about two-second intervals and clicking or clucking to encourage him to go forwards. The squeezing would be about as strong as I could make it without actually kicking. I would do it by closing my legs with increasing strength. This means that he can choose to respond at any time and I stop squeezing. If I get to the end of my squeeze and he still hasn't moved, I release the pressure and start again ... and again, repeating the process until he either gives in or I know he isn't going to.

The truly stubborn horse who resists all efforts to get him going needs to go right back to basics to have his whole attitude changed (see Chapter 14).

SUMMARY

Refusing to go forwards is usually a vote of no confidence.
Possible reasons are:
- ❖ He hasn't been there before and lacks confidence. Introduce things slowly and carefully.
- ❖ He has been there before and doesn't want to repeat the experience. Lower expectations and make it easy for him.
- ❖ He doesn't like the look of what's in front of him. See Chapter 5.
- ❖ The rider is holding him in/hanging onto his head. Sit with confidence and loosen the reins.
- ❖ The rider is nervous/insecure. Put the rider on a leading-rein or a different horse.
- ❖ The riding style doesn't suit him. Play around with leg/rein contact.

Alternatively, he is spoilt, stubborn and knows he can get away with it: learn the art of squeezing.

Treat each situation on its own merits: the truly stubborn horse needs to go right back to basics.

11. SPINNING ROUND

The wild horse uses spinning round to effect the fastest possible change of direction. Something very threatening has just appeared in front of him. His best defence is to run the other way. Nature has equipped him with speed and agility. He can, if necessary, turn on a sixpence.

WHY HORSES SPIN ROUND

Among our own horses, the one who spins without warning is a canny one and quick on his feet, but the root of spinning round is the same as stopping and not wanting to go forward. The threat of what lies ahead seems (to the horse) to be too big to contemplate. He's not having it. Essentially, he is that much more determined to have his own way. With luck on his side, he will get away with it and cart his rider back home.

From the horse's point of view, most commonly, the horse just wants to go back home and will do whatever it takes to get there. More often than not, he lacks confidence in his rider. Sometimes he spins round because he knows he can get away with it. Sometimes he puts in a quick rear before the spin, to make the point that he is absolutely not going on. If he unseats the rider, so much the better for him! He's free to do what he wants!

DEALING WITH SPINNING ROUND

If confronted by this issue, if possible, I block the spin. As quick as a flash, I open the opposite hand out wide and pull heavily on it. At the same time, I apply the same-side leg to bend him round it.

Once the spin has been blocked and the horse has accepted the discipline, I carry on as if nothing has happened. This is important. Like the horse, we must be forgiving. If he spins again, I would of course deal with it in the same way.

However, there are horses who are simply too quick, strong and agile. Blocking their spin is impossible. In this case, I follow him through and make him continue the spin into a full circle. This is easily done. He is turning anyway – I just make him turn some more.

When we get back to facing

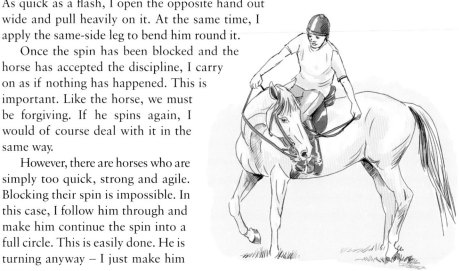

Try to block the spin if possible.

the direction I want him to go, I squeeze him on firmly, usually with a strongly voiced 'WALK ON' to reinforce my intentions. He may or may not oblige. It depends how determined he is. He may spin again, although this rarely happens. More often, he simply plants his feet and says 'I won't!' If this happens, I have to assess the situation.

As we now know, horses dislike conflict. As a general rule, it only makes them worse. The better part of valour may be to dismount and lead the horse through his block, or it may be better to drive him strongly forwards, putting extra pressure on the appropriate rein to prevent him from spinning again. It all depends on how strong and quick the horse is – and your own ability. Always take the easy route, if you're not sure.

The question must also be asked – why would he prefer to go home, or get back to his mates, or simply away from here? Am I expecting too much, or making him work too hard? Spinning round is an extension of refusing to go forwards. The reasons for both are the same.

Where the horse is 'having you on' because you lack the skill or confidence, you may be well advised to put yourself on the leading-rein, until you have established a better and more understanding relationship. Alternatively, allowing the horse to follow freely behind another steady, reliable horse is another option. Either way, you need to develop your riding skills and find the necessary confidence.

In the worst-case scenario, where nothing works, the horse may need some serious retraining to change his attitude. The best I can do here is to explain what we did with Ellie.

A retraining programme

Among many other tricks, Ellie had spinning round down to a fine art. She would stop, rear and spin so fast that the rider didn't have a chance. Turning the full circle didn't make much difference. She would simply do it again, or plant her feet and refuse point-blank to move.

Ellie's problem stemmed from always getting away with refusing to hack out. She would go a short distance down the road or track, and then start her shenanigans. It worked every time.

Her basic problem was with leaving home. It simply wasn't on her agenda, so the first step was to lead her out in hand. She was still resistant, but less so. She always stopped at the same place, but using the 'equal and opposite' leading technique, it wasn't so difficult to get her going again. Once we had overcome that block, she gave in completely and behaved very well.

The next step was to give her the reassurance of going out in company, tapping in to wild-horse herd instinct. As she was so flighty, we started with 'ride and lead'. I rode and led her off another horse, while my daughter Jess rode along behind to 'shoo' her forward, if necessary. She took to that very well and forgot about stopping at her favourite place.

So far, so good, but she still hadn't been ridden, so this was the next step. Again, it was carefully managed. The toss-up was whether to put a companion horse in front or behind. Would she follow the leader, or would her determination to return to her old tricks come to the surface?

We opted to put the companion horse behind for two reasons. The first was that if she stopped, Jess could come up from behind and drive her forward, with a touch from a whip, if necessary. The second reason was about hacking out alone, which was the ultimate goal. When a horse can take the lead in company and without a bum to follow, he is responsible for himself. With a mare like Ellie, this is a useful step forward.

The judgement was sound. The company of one other horse, albeit behind her, was enough to reassure her. She went very well. Stopping, rearing and spinning round had, for the time being, been forgotten – but we had one more hurdle to cross.

She was hacked out a few times with the same companion horse, until we felt she was ready to go it alone. What would she do? We didn't know until we tried it. Somewhat to our disappointment, she did what she had always done before, but without the spinning round. She stopped and refused to go forwards. There was only one solution – she had to be driven from behind.

As she was ridden away from the gate, I stood ready with a lunge whip held behind my back and pointing down to the ground. As she went past, I raised the lunge whip and cracked it behind her. That changed her mind. With something else to think about, she forgot her resistance and surged forward into trot. Jess let her go. Ellie going on without stopping was just what Jess wanted. No matter that she went away in trot. That was not a problem!

The next couple of times that Jess hacked out, I stood ready with the lunge whip but it was no longer needed. Elle never tried seriously to resist going out alone again. If she ever did, all we would have had to do would have been to repeat the procedure.

From here, Ellie was hacked out mostly on her own, but sometimes in company for reassurance. She did sometimes revert to her stop/rear/spin routine, but it was quickly dealt with (by following through and circling) and ultimately, she knew better than to argue. Eventually, she stopped even trying.

SUMMARY
❖ When possible, block the spin.
❖ Otherwise, follow through on the circle, until the horse is facing the right way.
❖ Drive forward strongly. Block another spin on the appropriate rein.
❖ Dismounting and leading forward may be the best option.
❖ Ask yourself the right questions.
❖ If necessary, put yourself on a leading-rein, or allow your horse to follow freely behind another horse.
❖ Retraining may be needed.

12. HEAD-SHAKING

The origin of shaking or tossing the head about is flies, which have almost certainly been around since the dawn of the horse. It is the horse's defence mechanism against them. We see it all the time in summer; swishing tails and nodding heads as they doze peacefully under a shady tree. This tells us that both swishing the tail and shaking the head are signs of irritation.

RESPONSE TO DISCOMFORT IN THE MOUTH

From the horse's point of view, a horse doing this is irritated or mildly annoyed. Shaking or tossing the head about while being ridden is telling us that the horse has an irritation. It is most likely to be in his mouth. He has this bit in there, which is simply uncomfortable. There might be various reasons for this, but the most likely one is that there is too much pressure on it (which, of course, will exacerbate any other causes of discomfort). Like flies buzzing round his head, the bit is nagging in his mouth.

Along with nagging at his mouth, we are also prone to nagging with our legs, keeping them closed to 'push' him along and keep him going. Meanwhile, the horse is thinking, 'I know what I'm doing. You don't have to keep reminding me'. And we all know how irritating it is to be nagged at all the time. By tossing his head around, he is trying to rid himself of this irritation.

DEALING WITH HEAD-SHAKING

With a horse who has got into this habit who, from the feel of him and the way he rides generally, I know can be trusted, I wouldn't do anything more than loosen the reins, to make him comfortable in the mouth. He won't do anything daft like run away. I also know that when I ask him to slow down or stop, he will respond as I want him to.

As you can see in the adjacent photos, having made no attempt to control the unsteadiness in the mare's head, Jess has loosened the reins and given the mare what she wanted; within a second

FROM MY CASE BOOK

Jody was a chronic head-shaker. His owner said she had tried everything, although I don't know what 'everything' was. All I knew was that he suffered from too much control on the reins.

He was the kindest, most placid and obliging little horse imaginable. I sensed this as soon as I got on his back. I took him home and put him into every imaginable situation to persuade him to shake his head. Naturally, he was given a loose, comfortable rein.

Only once, trotting along a grass verge, did he give the tiniest shake of his head, as if a memory had been triggered and he felt he ought to. That was the end of it. He was sold on to a teenager, who loved him to bits.

NB: It does appear that nowadays, some horses can be irritated by things in the air such as pollen and tiny midges which are invisible to us. In these cases, trying to 'solve' the problem by restraint with the reins will make it much worse. However, a protective nose-net has often been found to be effective: a simple solution that can work like a charm. Before spending money, do check first that the problem is not caused by too tight a rein. In most cases of unsteadiness in the head, releasing the reins is the simple solution!

or two, she is back to normal.

Actually, most horses can be trusted, if we only give them the chance. And trust is a two-way thing. When we show the horse we trust him, he knows he can trust us. But we have to go first. By riding him, we put ourselves in the position of leader. In asking him to do what we want, we lead the way. In areas like trust and confidence, we show by example.

It is true that some horses inspire trust and confidence and others don't. But we must always give them the benefit of the doubt. We will find out soon enough if they have any problems in this department.

Loosening the contact may be all that is required.

SUMMARY

❖ The origin of head-shaking is defence against flies.
❖ When ridden, it is a sign of irritation, usually in the mouth.
❖ Loosen the reins.
❖ Show the horse by example that you trust him.
❖ Always give the benefit of the doubt.
❖ With head-shaking induced by external irritants, a nose-net can be effective.

13. LEANING ON THE BIT/PULLING

This is a clear case of 'equal and opposite reaction'. The horse will only pull or snatch at the reins, or lean on the bit, when there is something to lean on or pull against. It's rather like a tug-of-war. Each side (horse and rider) pulls against the other in the hope of winning or, in this case, getting what they want.

WHY HORSES LEAN OR PULL

From the horse's point of view, the reins are too short or tight, making the horse uncomfortable in his mouth. He responds by trying to pull his head away from this discomfort. In effect, he is asking very politely, 'Would you please let go of the reins. I know what I'm doing and you can trust me. I'm not going to run away or do anything stupid.'

The horse is actually very well behaved. He walks along obediently and trots when asked. But something is bothering him. That something is the constant pressure in his mouth. In all likelihood, this horse needs no reins at all to keep him on the straight and narrow. Leave him alone and he will just get on with the job.

Under normal circumstances, the horse can be trusted to do what he has been trained to do. It is only our intervention that makes his behaviour abnormal. Thus we must always trust the horse, unless we have good reason not to. When we first take on a new horse, we are entitled to be cautious, but the more we get to know each other, the more we can relax our guard. And the quicker we do this, the better.

What we must not do is ride robotically. We must not pick up the reins, clamp our legs to his sides and expect the horse to get on with it. We must be sensitive to his personal preferences and the degree to which he accepts or tolerates leg and/or rein contact. When you ride a horse for the first time, play around with both, to find out what keeps him happy and comfortable.

Find the rein contact with which the horse is comfortable.

DEALING WITH LEANING AND PULLING

When hacking

Above all, it is important for the horse to be comfortable and relaxed. He can only do this when nothing is bothering him. Therefore, I would loosen off the reins, until I find the point where he stops leaning or pulling. I would then know when he is comfortable. As with shaking or throwing his head around, I show trust, allowing him to get on with what he is supposed to be doing. As there is nothing at the other end to pull against, he stops leaning on the bit or pulling at the reins immediately.

When schooling

In a schooling situation, the horse's message is the same. He is still saying, 'The reins are too short/tight. I am uncomfortable in the mouth. Please give me my head.' What you do here depends on what you are trying to achieve. If you want to just walk, trot and canter round the arena, to give the horse some exercise, give the horse what he wants. Play around with your rein contact, until you find the place where he is comfortable.

If, in the other hand, you are aiming to progress his training in the higher disciplines, you probably need to strengthen your leg aids and ride him more strongly into the bridle. Riding 'between hand and leg' is a sensitive business. You need to get the balance just right. If this is what you are aiming to do, work your way towards the stronger contact carefully and gradually. Listen to the horse and read the signs. He'll tell you if you are overdoing it.

Context and interpretation

NB: *Please do remember that, **from the horse's point of view**, hacking and schooling are two entirely distinct and separate activities. Hacking is (or should be) for relaxation. Schooling is for learning specific lessons and/or progressing training.*

It is so important to look at what the horse is doing and interpret the action. If the horse could talk, what would he say? Some actions are easier to interpret than others. This one couldn't be easier. He is saying, 'Please leave my mouth alone. I know what I'm doing.' End of story!

SUMMARY
❖ Listen to what the horse is saying.
❖ Be sensitive to his personal preferences.
❖ Make him comfortable in the mouth.
❖ Trust him to do what he has been trained to do.
❖ When schooling, stronger leg aids may be needed.
❖ Sometimes, more is to be gained by letting the horse have his way.

EXPERT TIP

If your horse pulls his head down or away quite forcefully, let the reins slip through your fingers. More is to be gained by momentarily letting him have his way. When he reaches the end of his neck-stretch, simply ask him to bring his head back up again.

Notice how, in the photo, Jess just sits still and does nothing, allowing Elle to drop her head. This says to Ellie that she is not worried about it. Neither does she engage in any kind of fight.

14. THE STUBBORN, SPOILT HORSE

Horses are no fools. If we don't ask with enough conviction, they simply say, 'No thanks!' and do whatever they choose to do. A horse like this quickly takes on the characteristics of the spoilt child. Some things he will do very nicely – if it suits him. He will usually, for example, come in gaily for his bucket. He may even stand quietly to be groomed and tacked up. But ask him to go for a ride or do something else he'd rather not do and he digs in his toes and says, 'I won't!'

Spoiling the horse by being too soft and giving in too easily can lead to a myriad problems. Horses need to know that we are in charge and we mean what we say – as long as it's reasonable and within the sphere of their experience. They also need to know the boundaries of what is acceptable and what is not. Overall, disobedience is not acceptable. The stubborn horse needs to be straightened out.

DEALING WITH STUBBORN/SPOILT HORSES

The stubborn horse is so far removed from the natural basic nature of horses that he has little or no desire to cooperate. Which approach I take with such a horse depends on the severity of the problem and the horse's past experience.

The worst-case scenario

In the worst-case scenario, I would go right back to basics and start with training the horse to basic obedience and voice commands on the lunge. This horse is often dead to everything and responds to neither leg nor rein.

I use a headcollar for lungeing but make sure that it fits snugly to the horse's head. I then attach the lunge rein to the ring on the side on which I am working. If the horse tries to pull away, which a stubborn horse is likely to do, he gets the clearest possible signal from the pressure exerted on the opposite side.

A headcollar used for lungeing should fit snugly.

The first achievable target

Before he can do anything else, he must learn to walk round more or less in a circle. I don't worry too much about how correct it is. I simply want to establish the principle. He is resistant. He doesn't want to do this. He wants to go back to his field and play. I drive him forwards with my lunge whip and use my voice a lot, telling him firmly to walk on and giving praise when he gets it right. Slowly, he starts to understand that he must do as he's told.

The horse must first learn to walk in a circle.

The second achievable target

When he is reasonable in walk, I bring him into halt, if I can get it. With a rider, the stubborn horse is only too willing to stop in the hope that the rider will dismount and that's the end of riding. On the lunge, he may adopt a more normal attitude of indifference and continue walking. If firm, clear voice commands and dropping the point of the lunge whip towards the ground are not enough, I will add a few short tugs on the rein.

The next stage is to teach him to halt.

If this fails, I will bring him in on a tight circle and continue with very firm voice commands combined with tugs on the rein until he understands and does what I want. This is about obedience and I want him to understand that. As long as he stands still for two or three moments, the principle is established and I'm happy.

The third achievable target

By now, he is beginning to get the message and answers to 'Walk on' and 'Stand'. I move him on into trot. Given that all horses prefer not to do anything energetic, the spoilt, stubborn horse is likely to be even more resistant. I get a definite 'I don't like doing this' response. He niggles. He tries to get away. I persevere, not asking for more than about half

Moving on to trot.

To improve control, it can be helpful to start on a very small circle.

a circuit at first. When I get one complete circuit, it's a triumph. We're on the way. Now I can work towards two circuits … and so on.

A handy tip for lungeing
The truly stubborn horse generally looks for any excuse to avoid doing what he's told.

Additionally, we have very little control when the horse is out at the end of a lunge rein. If he starts messing about there is not much we can do about it except stop and start again.

The answer is to start him off on a very small circle. As he understands what is wanted and settles to the idea, he is slowly given a longer rein. Equally, if he starts getting difficult on a full-length rein, I promptly bring him in close to me.

The fourth achievable target
When he answers reasonably well to 'Walk on', 'Trot on' and 'Halt', it's time to move on to riding. The first goal, as with lungeing, is basic obedience in walk. More often than not, he won't even stay on a straight line. Then he may pretend he's nervous and spooky. Anything to get out of this work!

To get his attention and keep his mind focused on me, I constantly make random circles, large and small, figures of eight and changes of rein. All this is done with the simple aids and using the lightest possible touch of the rein. It is perhaps surprising how light they become. You can almost hear the mind of such a horse ticking over: 'Well this is easy. I can do this!'

When progressing to riding, concentrate on keeping the horse's attention.

From time to time, I bring him to a halt. Most stubborn horses halt very easily under saddle; in part because it's what they want, preferably followed by the rider getting off. It's the getting going again which is more difficult. Now I want him to understand and respond to the lightest possible leg aid to go forward. At first, it may take quite a strong squeeze but after a few repetitions, he gets the idea and responds to the lightest touch.

From halt, the horse must learn to go forwards from a light aid.

The fifth achievable target

I get any small problems such as this more or less ironed out before moving on to the next goal, which is trot. It is important not to make an issue out of his little resistances, but to keep him moving on. He is reluctant to trot at first. It's too much like hard work, but now he is beginning to understand that I mean what I say.

Reluctantly, he breaks into what is often a slow, shambling trot. That's fine. He's trotting. I don't push it, but allow him to slow back to walk very soon after he tells me he's had enough. Slowly, I extend his ability to trot for longer and continue with figures, circles and rein changes. And so we go on, taking one small step at a time. Each step of the way, slowly but surely, he becomes increasingly willing and obedient.

The great day comes when we can manage a canter. Cantering within the confines of an arena is hard for any horse and a perfect excuse for the stubborn horse to resist, so I prefer to do this on a hack. I set it up to make it easy for him by putting him behind another horse so he can follow the leader and do what the other horse does. As he breaks into canter, I give the canter aids with my legs so he makes the association that, when trotting, this is the signal to go into canter. This simple association is not hard for him to understand and creates a horse who responds to the lightest possible aids. You can also add a voice command, a click or a cluck for aural reinforcement. With the first horse I ever trained, I spontaneously used a shooshing sound which worked so well that I hardly had to use my legs at all.

The horse 'having you on'

This is the horse who I know will do as he's told, as long as I can get through to him. This horse has usually been pulled about and kicked until his ribs are sore. Making sure I am not preventing him from going forward by the reins, first, I try the squeezing technique (see Chapter 10). Sometimes this works. The horse is so shocked to find himself treated kindly that he agrees to do as I ask. If this is not the answer, it may be necessary to proceed as detailed in Tilly's case history overleaf.

FROM MY CASE BOOK

Tilly was spoilt rotten and redefined the word 'stubborn'. She was a serious non-starter. She had planting her feet and refusing to move down to a fine art. I took her right back to basics and put her on the lunge. She didn't think much of that either and resisted in almost every way possible. Her favourite trick was to try to tank off whenever the circle took her in the direction of the gate. She soon found out that didn't work.

Slowly, but surely, she got the message and stopped messing about. Riding, however, was no easier. She niggled and spooked and looked for any excuse to stop. Happily, it was just possible to get through to her with repeated squeezing. I squeezed that mare until I had no more squeeze left in my legs.

Like many spoilt, stubborn horses, her walk was very slow. Even so, I could tell when slow started getting even slower and knew that Tilly was about to stop. On came the legs, squeezing forwards. At the same time, I would tell her sharply, 'WALK ON Tilly. Walk on!' Somewhere in the back of her brain, the desire to cooperate was just about alive. The pace would increase just enough to let me know that she wasn't going to stop – for now.

In between, I left her alone to get on with it. I gave her a loose, free rein and kept my legs still. In this way, she was going forward

of her own free will ... until she changed her mind. As time went by, the need to keep reminding her to keep going forward decreased. Eventually, she would also trot along until asked to return to walk. Having established obedience to trot, cantering wasn't so difficult. She resigned herself to it and loped along willingly enough. Finally, she turned into a normal riding horse.

SUMMARY
- ❖ The horse may need to be taken right back to basics.
- ❖ Train the horse to voice commands on the lunge.
- ❖ Establish obedience at each level before moving on.
- ❖ Take one very small step at a time.
- ❖ Expect progress to be very slow.

PART 3
HANDLING ON THE GROUND

We have touched on a few aspects of handling on the ground. Now we will consider them in more detail. What happens when we ride the horse, often impacts on his behaviour beforehand: if the horse's experience of riding is not a happy one, he may throw up all sorts of behaviour we don't like. Or, on the other hand, the behaviour may be entirely unconnected to riding. When the horse moves to a new home, he is often rather traumatised and all his previous good manners disappear – apparently into the abyss. We often underestimate just how unsettling moving to a new home can be. It is said of us that moving is one of life's major traumas: the same is often true for the horse.

As I have said before, problem behaviour does not appear out of nowhere. There is always a reason. First, we find the reason; then we take appropriate action.

From the horse's point of view, handling is not a problem – as long as he is used to whatever we want to do with him. Most horses get used to our demands and expectations in the first two or three years of life. They discover that, although some things we ask are (to them) a little bizarre, no harm comes from them. For example, standing on three legs, while we fiddle about with each foot in turn, makes no sense to them, until they are used to it. Then it just becomes another fact of life.

Likewise, tying them up and making them stand still in one place isn't normal or natural for a horse. But once again, as long as no harm comes from it, they accept with their usual equanimity. Where it all goes pear-shaped is when something bad becomes associated with what is otherwise an acceptable task or activity. The trigger may be physical. What we do, or the way we do it, is not to their liking. More commonly, it is psychological. They are nervous, insecure, frightened or angry.

We find that almost all resistance to handling (whatever that resistance may be) relates to the natural instincts of the wild horse. Thus, to solve the problem, we must treat our horse as if he **IS** a wild horse. He may have been perfectly good before, but he has reverted to the wild state and must, once again get used to it – slowly, gently and easily.

15. WON'T BE CAUGHT

Perhaps the most singular characteristic of the wild horse is that he won't be caught. He will tolerate our presence at a distance, but move in too close and he's off, running in the opposite direction. He does this purely for self-protection. He suspects that our motives are predatory and is not prepared to find out. On the bottom line, it is lack of trust and confidence.

WINNING TRUST AND CONFIDENCE

There is, however, a way to win horses' trust and confidence, regardless of this inherent fear. We see it with people who study wild animals, such as gorillas, monkeys, wolves, bears and so on. These are all sociable animals, with a capacity for friendship among themselves.

All we have to do is behave like a horse, showing respect for their fear and extreme caution in our approach. We only move in closer when the horse allows it. We wait patiently for permission and read the signs. He will only show acceptance when we prove that we are friendly and are not going to hurt or frighten him.

It is just as easy to win the trust of a group of wild horses as a band of jungle gorillas. It just takes time, patience, observation and understanding. When our horses become difficult to catch, they have 'gone wild' or reverted to the wild state and need much the same level of patience, observation and understanding. They have become wary and suspicious, so the question is – of what? There are so many possibilities that this becomes the million-dollar question.

From the horse's point of view, the primary answer to this question is that he is fearful. If he allows himself to be caught, something bad will happen. This could be a number of things. He is going to be separated from his friends and companions. He is insecure and doesn't like that. He is going to be ridden. He doesn't like that either. Or, the worst-case scenario, he's going to be loaded into a horsebox and taken to another place. A horse may be hard to catch soon after arriving at a new home. He is afraid he might be moved again. One upheaval is bad enough, but two in quick succession is intolerable. Or maybe something bad happened the day before and he is afraid of it being repeated.

If horses feel threatened, they instinctively move away.

It can be that he doesn't like the look of the person approaching. Highly tuned to it, he senses danger. In comes the flight reflex. He runs away. His fear is quickly reinforced. We go into predator mode and go after him. We keep on coming, following wherever he goes.

His wild-horse instincts are now on full alert. He may know us very well, but that doesn't make any difference. He does not rationalise. He simply reacts. He has a reason for running away and that reason now is that he doesn't want to be caught. Behind his objection is another reason – but we will come to that. For now, he sees himself as the prey and us as the predator. We may be smaller than him, but that's irrelevant. For now, he sees himself threatened: instinctively, he moves away from the threat.

How to proceed

The task here is to regain his trust and confidence. I use the 'stop and wait' technique, which replicates natural horse behaviour. As soon as I see him, which may be before I even go through the gate, I start watching him carefully. He will do the same, lifting his head and watching me intently. He is now in wild-horse mode. He wants to know what I am going to do. I read the signs so that I can act accordingly.

The first achievable target

My first goal, if possible, is to stop him turning away. How do I do this? As soon as I see him gathering himself up to make a move, I stop and wait. Now, he's not so much scared as curious. What am I going to do next?

In the photo, Rhia is watching me intently. What am I going to do next? At the same time, I am watching her. I am looking at her head, ears and legs. Does she look as if she is poised to turn away? Is she thinking about it? I wait until her body language tells me that she is not going to move – just yet. Her attention is on me, with her ears pricked forward, and she is standing squarely.

Watching and waiting.

The second achievable target

I wait a moment while we establish our positions and then take a step or two forward, watching just as carefully as before. At the first sign of unease,

I stop and wait again and repeat the procedure. In standing still and doing nothing, fear is replaced by curiosity. By my behaving like a horse, the horse begins to feel he can trust me. Slowly, I proceed until finally, I get up to him.

The third achievable target

Having got up to the horse, I now want to show that I am kind and friendly. I reward liberally with pony nuts. Taking my time, I stop and give him some petting and patting, to let him know that I am not in a hurry. Horses hate to be rushed. If I know in advance that the horse is going to be difficult, he will already have a headcollar on. If not, I quietly slip the rope round his neck in the course of my petting and patting. Now he knows he is caught and that's the end of it.

NB: When I turn a new horse out, I always leave the headcollar on for a few days. I don't know how he is going to respond to me, or his new home, and I want to make the catching process as easy as possible.

I may have to repeat this procedure a few times, until he is fully trusting and confident that I am not going to upset him in any way. If there are other issues connected with his unwillingness to be caught, I'll be addressing those as well.

When it isn't so easy

Where it gets sticky is when the horse is so nervous that he turns and runs off in another direction. Wild-horse mode goes one step further. Instinct tells him to first run away, then stop and check out the situation. As soon as he sees me, he starts moving away in the opposite direction, usually in walk. I stop and wait for him to stop moving, because I know that, sooner or later, he will stop and look at me to see what I am doing.

If he has gone quite some distance, I walk slowly and carefully towards him, watching for the sign that he is going to run off again. Then I stop and wait. Such a horse usually does run off a few times. I repeat the procedure, going so far in his direction then stopping to let him know that I am not going to chase him. Slowly, we build a rapport. He begins to trust me and allows me to come closer. I know now that I am on the winning ticket.

After about fifteen minutes or so, most horses get tired of playing cat and mouse. It's a tedious game really, because he has to keep running away and waste his precious energy. Besides, it's not getting him anywhere. He gives in. He allows me to come right up to him. I give him much praise, tell him what a good boy he is and slip the rope round his neck.

The essence lies in your inner stillness and being totally in control of yourself. Every move you make is quiet and restrained. The state of inner stillness shows no fear and acts as a perfect foil for the horse's troubled mind. He can respond to and respect it. Additionally, you are showing by example what you want, which is peace and harmony. You let the horse know that you intend to succeed, rather than trying to impose your will upon him.

A useful ploy

A useful ploy is to hide the headcollar behind your back. Horses can easily be fooled – if you go the right way about it. As often as not, it is the sight of the headcollar that sends the horse running. He may not be able to rationalise very much, but he knows what a headcollar means.

Offering a treat can also be a useful ploy – but the same procedure of 'stop/wait/watch/advance and wait again' must be followed. The horse is not that easily fooled. However, it is interesting to watch how his attention is often focused on the hand holding out the treat. He wants it really, but does he dare take it? Not until we have made all the right moves first.

When you get close enough, you must NOT make a grab for him. He still has the freedom of choice and is likely to wheel away at the slightest provocation. Give the treat, if it is offered, then move quietly towards the side of his head.

Reach over or under his neck (whichever is more convenient) and slide the hand firmly down the far side. Give a little pat and tell him he's a good boy. Essentially, with the rope round his neck, he is now caught and most horses know it.

In the adjacent photos, notice my inner stillness throughout. I take my time, moving in the way that horses like. There is no rush or hurry. Everything is done very calmly and quietly. Any sign of panic or anxiety and the horse will be off like a shot. Notice also my close proximity to the horse. First, the closer I am, the more

Top: Offering a treat can be useful.
Middle to bottom: The right approach is to be quiet and unhurried.

control I have. Second, it gives a sense of reassurance. Standing at arm's length suggests nervousness or uncertainty and we want the horse, above all, to feel secure.

Put the headcollar on from the side, not from in front of the horse.

NB: *We train all our horses to believe that they are caught as soon as they feel the hand on the far side of the neck. This has proved incredibly useful on many occasions when a horse has had a moment of doubt.*

We also make a habit of putting the headcollar on from the side of the horse's head, rather than directly in front of it, as this is a much less threatening approach – and has also paid dividends with a horse who is thinking about running away. The point is that we never take any horse for granted.

The plastic bag game!

This technique is for the horse who is really nervous about being caught. Armed with a good supply of pony nuts or similar in a plastic bag, you start by persuading him to accept treats off your hand without any intention of catching him. The first goal is to engage him in the game, so you keep replenishing the treats in your hand until he is actively looking for more.

You may find that, as you reach into the plastic bag, the sound of it startles him slightly and he turns away. Just hold out your hand with the treats, stay very still and wait for him to come back again.

If necessary, make yourself less threatening by sitting down on the ground. Hold out the treats and wait for him to come to you. So often, it is tempting to go after the horse but this is precisely what drives him away. If, on the other hand, you stay where you are, his natural curiosity and/or his interest in yummy treats draws him closer.

When he has had, say, three or four offerings, very quietly turn and walk away. If you are lucky, he will come after you. If this happens, walk on a little way and then stop, turn and reward him with some more treats. (This is Join-up by any other name!) You can repeat this as often as you like, leading him all around the field if you want to.

If you are less lucky, he will stand and watch you walk away but that's OK. You carry on and leave it for that day. You still have a lot of trust-building to do. Try again the next day. There is no hurry. It won't be long before he starts thinking, 'This is a good game. I like it. All I have to do is follow and I get good things to eat.' At the same time, he comes to associate the sound of the rustling plastic bag with a good reward. Later on, all you have to do is rustle the plastic bag and he comes to you.

The name of this game is patience. All too often we are in too much of a hurry. Our instincts drive us to get to the goal as quickly as possible. By contrast, the horse is all caution and suspicion. To win any game with the horse, we have to play it his way.

The truly wild horse

From time to time, we come across a horse who appears to be truly wild and won't let us come anywhere near him. This is usually a youngster who has not had a good experience of people. On principle, he distrusts all of them.

WHAT I WOULD DO

The easiest procedure is to work with him in a pen or stable for about two weeks which does first mean catching him or rounding him up by any means possible.

The plastic bag game.
1. Start by persuading the horse to accept treats, with no intention of catching him.
2. Sitting down can make you appear less threatening.
3. After a few offerings, turn and walk away.
4. If the horse follows you, stop and reward him.

The first achievable target

Before anything else can be achieved, he must accept my presence. I go into the pen/stable and make myself comfortable. All I am going to do is spend time with him, doing nothing at all. From time to time, I will say a few soft words: 'Well there's a good boy. Come on then. Let's be having you ...' Mostly, it's nonsense, but that doesn't matter. Eventually, he stops cowering in the corner and starts showing curiosity.

The second achievable target

Next, I want him to accept a hand-held treat. I have one ready. I don't move, but maintain inner stillness and wait for him to come to me. I hold the treat out on the palm of my hand. Cautiously, he sniffs it. When he feels enough trust and confidence, he takes it. Softly, I tell him what a good boy he is. I give him a few more treats; then I go.

The third achievable target

On the assumption that this horse has been handled before, I now want him to know that my touch is kind and considerate. When he willingly accepts my presence and takes treats from my hand, I start looking for places he likes to be rubbed or scratched, as a prelude to grooming. By now, he is feeling quite confident with me, and beginning to behave like a normal horse. We are becoming friends. Slowly, but surely, his reservations are broken down, until my presence and hands on him are totally acceptable. Within a week or so, I find him waiting for me in happy anticipation of good things to come.

The fourth achievable target

At this point, I practise putting the headcollar on and taking it off again – all done very slowly and gently. I would give much praise and reward him every step of the way. I want this horse to find the whole experience a pleasurable one.

The fifth achievable target

The next step is to take him out and lead him about a bit. If there is some grass in the vicinity (a bank or verge, for example) I will be a good friend and take him grazing. This will be the one thing he wants more than anything else. And what a pleasure it is to watch him wrapping his teeth round some nice, juicy grass.

The sixth achievable target

After a couple of weeks, I turn him out with a headcollar on. I want his first catching experience, when loose in the field, to be as easy as possible. By now, he is pleased to see me, and approaches of his own accord. He gets the treat he expects and we are still friends.

UNDERLYING ISSUES

Having caught the horse, we must also consider what might be wrong in the bigger picture. What is the underlying cause of this behaviour?

New home syndrome

As mentioned, moving to a new home can be traumatic for a horse. His familiar field, companions, stable, routine, rider and the people around him have all gone. Everything is new, strange and different. He is wary. He doesn't know what to expect. If he is more nervous than the average horse, or has had bad experience in the past, he may choose to avoid all further contact with people.

It is always a good idea therefore, to spend the first day or two just making some friendly visits and asking for nothing more than his acceptance of us. We can see on the first approach how friendly he is going to be. Does he look suspicious, or merely curious? Does he allow us to walk up to him? Or does he give us the wary eye and turn his head away? Depending on his response to the sight of us, we approach accordingly.

Horses keep their greetings short and sweet.

Once again, we take our cue from how horses greet each other. They keep it short and sweet. 'Sweet' to them may involve squealing and pawing the ground, but once the greeting is over, they return to what they were doing before. In the photo, notice the caution of Tiggy (on the left), ears back, indicating to Dolly (right) that she takes nothing for granted.

WHAT I WOULD DO

The essence then is to keep these meetings short. I would make no attempt to catch the horse, but would offer a few treats (if it seems appropriate) and some friendly petting – but not too much of that either. Too many treats can make the horse greedy, which in turn can lead to aggressive behaviour.

Horses don't go much for petting. It doesn't mean anything to them, but a good rub or scratch under the mane or round the base of the ears is often appreciated. Thus, the new horse learns that we are good to know and so he will lower his guard next time.

If, on the other hand, he turns tail and walks away, I know I have to work at cultivating his trust and friendship and go through the stop/wait/watch/advance procedure. I keep on doing this, taking note of progress, until he allows me to catch him normally. Additionally, I would take this as a warning sign that I might have to tread carefully later on. His lack of trust and confidence may go deeper.

Fear of separation (separation anxiety)

This and New Home Syndrome are often linked. The horse allows himself to be caught, but discovers there is a price to pay. He is taken away from his new-found friends and companions. This is most likely to happen when there are only two of them. The wild-horse need for company is so strong that two horses sharing a field bond like no other. Separating one from his only field-mate seems like the end of the world. Again, he cannot rationalise that they will be reunited. It is the here and now that matters and it bothers him immensely.

From the horse's point of view, the next day, he says to himself, 'There's no way I'm going to let that happen again!' and off he goes at the first sight of us. This horse has to learn that separation is not the end of the world and, in any case, it's only temporary. In due course, he is reunited. However, as this fear is rooted so deeply in his psyche, this is a long, slow lesson. In the meantime, he is likely to show a lot of anxiety during separation.

The more anxious he gets, the less he learns. If he gets too wound up, he is consumed by it and is soon close to panic. There are no lessons to be learned from panic, other than to emphasise and reinforce an unpleasant experience.

WHAT I WOULD DO

Here, 'achievable targets' are determined by the horse's response. I start with taking him as far as he is willing to go. At first, I may only take him as far as the gate, spend a minute or so making a bit of a fuss of him, then turn him loose again. When this is acceptable, I would take him through the gate and increasingly further away from his field. Along the way, I would be watching carefully for signs of anxiety.

Take the horse just as far as he's willing to go, then make a fuss of him.

Reading the signs

He will show me he's anxious by getting fidgety. He may start to jog, or turn his head, trying to look backwards at where he wants to go – which is, of course, back to his companion(s). Now, I would assess the situation. How deep is his anxiety? How far can I push him? In any event, I would take him on a little bit further. Where he goes must be my decision, not his. But having obtained a little more acquiescence, I give in and give him what he wants. I take him back to the field. 'Phew!' he says, 'Thank goodness for that!' but on further reflection, he understands. That wasn't so bad after all.

How to continue

Slowly, I extend the boundary, taking him further and for a little longer, giving much praise along the way. It can't be proved, but I believe a horse likes appreciation for his efforts. In any case, showing appreciation makes us feel good – which is never a bad thing.

The essence here is to give in when the horse's anxiety level rises. Basically, he is saying, 'I've had enough. I can't take any more.' This is another form of 'give and take' … or maybe 'take and give'. We take as much as the horse is willing to give and then give him what he wants. And so we go on, slowly building trust in us, and the confidence that he will be reunited with his friends.

With a new horse, we must always read the signs and act accordingly. Take him for granted and he will bite back, one way or another.

The day before

The horse has always been easy to catch and then one day, seemingly out of the blue, he isn't. What has got into his head? Since he can't tell us, we have to work it out and the first thing to look at is what happened the day before. Was he taken away from home, to a show or competition perhaps? He may have been very well behaved, but that doesn't mean he liked it. Or he may have found it stressful and visibly had a hard time. Either way, he thinks, 'I'm not going to fall for that again!'

Maybe you've had an uncharacteristic argument, or asked him to do something he didn't like very much. Nine times out of ten, when the horse suddenly won't be caught, there is a connection with what happened the day before.

WHAT I WOULD DO

If the experience is likely to be repeated, such as a show or competition, I would simply deal with the situation in whatever way works. I would hide the headcollar, tempt him with a bucket, or simply use the 'stop and wait' technique. The horse will have to get used to doing these things – which he should, in due course.

If something bad happened that was preventable, I work out what it was and take steps to prevent it from happening again. I may, uncharacteristically, have lost my temper, had a fight, or an argument. Perhaps I pushed him too hard, asked for too much. These are all very human things to do. There is no need to reproach yourself for stepping over the edge – but we can try to make sure it doesn't happen again.

Everything the horse does is telling us what is going on his mind. We have to act as interpreter and translate his thoughts and feelings into our own words. Sometimes, it isn't easy but, in effect, the horse is always giving us the answer.

GENERAL ADVICE

The following tips can be generally useful when dealing with horses who are, or have been, hard to catch.

Bribery

Make a habit of giving your horse a little treat every time you catch him. (I use pony nuts or similar feed such as cool cubes or pencils as they are not too sweet. Things like carrots and Polos can make a horse greedy, which in turn can make him pushy, and you don't want that.) Offer the treat before you put the headcollar on so he can munch it quietly while you get on with the job. There is nothing quite like bribery to encourage the horse stay with you.

If the horse is new to you, give him a treat when you turn him out as well, thus leaving him literally with a good taste in his mouth. When you next appear, his thoughts will turn immediately to the good things that come out of your pocket. As time goes by and he becomes amenable, you can dispense with treats altogether.

Using a catch-rope.

A cunning little ploy

Leave about an arm's length of rope attached to the headcollar. I call it a 'catch-rope'. The scary moment for a timid horse is the hand coming up close to his head to take hold of the headcollar. Leaving a bit of rope dangling means that you can catch hold of him so gently that he doesn't notice.

Don't worry about him tripping himself up on it, or anything like that. He will probably step on it once or twice but will soon learn how to work the rope and avoid it.

Making yourself smaller can improve your chances of success.

Make yourself smaller

This is a handy little trick. The smaller you are, the less threatening to the horse. In fact, when you do this, horses usually become downright inquisitive, as Chelsea demonstrates in the accompanying photos. Notice how her pony drops his head as if to say, 'What are you doing down there?'

SUMMARY

❖ The horse goes into wild-horse mode and must be treated accordingly.
❖ The 'stop and wait' technique replicates natural horse behaviour.
❖ Read the signs and act accordingly.
❖ Standing still and doing nothing replaces fear with curiosity.
❖ New Home Syndrome – make friends with the horse.
❖ Fear of separation – increase time and distance incrementally.
❖ Trouble the day before – use any method described above that works. The horse has to get used to it.
❖ Through his behaviour, the horse is always giving us the right answer.

FROM MY CASE BOOK

More about Pudsie. I bought her as a four-year-old, allegedly halter broken. The implication was that she had at least been handled and was used to people. Certainly, on arrival, she was quiet enough to lead from the trailer to the field. I turned her out with the group, as I always do with a new horse. There was no way she was going to be caught again. Every trick in the book failed miserably.

After about three months, there was only one way to go. We used a mare who had befriended her as a decoy and tricked her into a pen. In the pen, she was introduced to pony nuts in a bucket. It was fairly obvious that she had never seen a bucket before, let alone found out that it might contain some tasty food. Catching her in the pen was easy enough. She simply gave in. Once caught, she was no trouble at all.

Using the other mare as a decoy became the preferred method of catching her, until the mare was no longer needed and she allowed herself to be caught normally. We were always aware though, that we had to tread carefully. We could not take Pudsie for granted.

She was fine for the next two or three years. I broke her to riding, which wasn't so easy. She was such a nervous little horse. Then, one day, seemingly out of the blue, she decided she wasn't going to be caught. She ran off. I stopped to watch. What was she doing? Where was she going? Somewhat to my surprise, she ran round to the back of the group and stopped. 'Aha!', I thought, 'She's trying to hide.'

I cut through the middle of the group and headed slowly, but purposefully, towards her. Off she went again, circling the group, until she'd reached the opposite side. Then she stopped again. We continued this merry dance for about ten minutes. Then came the moment when she just gave in. I was somewhat to the rear, approaching obliquely from behind. I walked steadily up to her and put my hand on her rump. She stood for it. That was the end of it. I then caught her normally.

From time to time, she would pull the same trick again, but now we had a formula. We called it 'walking Puds'. It was no bother. We just knew

it would take five or ten minutes longer to catch her. She is now in her twenties and has a son, from whom she was only ever separated for about a year, when she went out on loan to a friend. She still has her occasional 'off' days, but all we do now is catch Dibley, her son. She comes trotting after him. 'Don't leave me', she says piteously. And then she catches normally.

16. WON'T LEAD IN HAND/ RUSHES WHEN LED

Many a problem starts because the horse is held too tight, too close, or as a result of specific ideas about where he should be positioned. The essence is to allow the horse to find his own position. This will be the one that suits him best.

Most people, whose job is working with horses, take a very casual attitude. The horse simply plods along behind them, each one fully trusting the other. As we have discovered, this fits in perfectly with the wild-horse instinct, which is to follow safely behind another. As you can see in the accompanying photo, the rope is loose and both pony and leader are simply getting on with the job. Notice the position of the pony's ears, which show that Milly is relaxed and submissive.

Some horses are not so cooperative. They have other issues, but we must always give them the chance to show their willing cooperation, as well as the freedom to make the right decision. If their choice is not to our liking, we must deal with it.

How often does the following happen? We go to lead the horse forward and he simply says, 'I won't!' Either he doesn't want to leave where he is (usually his field) or to go where we want to take him – usually away from home. Either way, he has nothing else to complain about.

From the horse's point of view, he is just trying to have his own way. From his point of view, refusing to move is always worth a try.

Above: When you see how horses are naturally prone to following one behind the other, you can see how leading from in front makes sense.
Top photo: When leading, allow the horse to find the position that suits him best.

DEALING WITH HORSES WHO WON'T BE LED

Such a horse often does have other issues, which must also be resolved, but in the short term he must learn to do as he's told. The first achievable target is to get him to take one or two steps forward. I start with 'give and take' on the rope.

Give and take

This means that I am going to give a little and take a little. I stand back a short distance, to give him space to think about it. I make the first move by pulling (taking) on the rope. He resists. He pulls against me. I give a little

and stop pulling, but keep the rope taut, creating 'an equal and opposite' reaction. The rope is just taut enough to let him know that I am still there and I want him to come with me – not backwards, or up, or anywhere else. As long as I keep the rope taut *but not tight* he will stay where he is.

Reading the signs

His head goes up. He holds it there. He's waiting to see what I'm going to do next. I do nothing, but stay where I am, holding the rope taut and watching him closely. Holding his head up like that is tedious, boring and tiring. I give a little, to let him know that he can bring his head back down to its normal position. This is a moment of submission, and also the moment to 'take'.

Top: The 'give and take' technique.
Above: As soon as the horse starts moving, release the pressure on the rope.

I pick up the pressure and pull, gently at first, then harder. I feel him resist. Do I give in, or insist? Usually, I insist, because I know the horse and know what I can get away with. I can feel it. As soon as he starts moving, I release the pressure on the rope. Now he is free to make the right decision. Nine times out of ten, it works. The horse takes at least one or two steps forward. One–nil to me!

The immediate result

This depends on the horse and the situation. Some horses will give in with only one of these little confrontations. They just need to assert themselves and make a point. However, if the point they want to make is a big one, they stop again and refuse to move. If this happens, the next achievable target is to move on a little further, by following the same procedure. We start all over again with the 'give and take' routine. And so we go on, until the horse gets the message and stops messing about.

Note that I use a long, loose lead-rope. This gives him the space to think freely for himself and to follow along as a wild horse would. If we make the experience of leading as kind and hassle-free as possible, he generally learns to accept it without making a fuss.

Most horses will succumb to this form of dialogue, but some are more determined than others. No amount of pulling and releasing the rope will persuade such a horse to uproot his feet and move. After two or three attempts with the 'give and take' technique, it becomes pretty obvious that he's not going to give in. I have to do something different.

Tricks of the trade
Change direction
Sometimes, when I find a horse so resistant that 'give and take' doesn't work, I have another trick up my sleeve. (I always try 'give and take' first, because it's the easiest and most natural.) But failing that, I turn next to 'changing direction'. This is a cunning little ploy, because it fools the horse into thinking he's going somewhere else. 'OK then', he says, 'If we're not going there, I'll come with you.'

Unfortunately, the horse works this ploy out pretty quickly. He says, 'Oh no. I get the idea. We're not really going somewhere else, are we?' Then he stops and plants his feet again. So once again, we either push or pull his head to turn away and face another direction. Hey presto! He's fooled again. He takes another two or three steps forward … and so we go on, until he's walking with us in whatever direction we find ourselves going. Two–nil to us, and not a fight in sight!

Thus the first objective, to get the horse going forward, even if only a step or two, has been achieved. We are getting what we want. The next achievable target is for the horse to take a few more steps in another direction. Slowly but surely, we proceed in a zigzag fashion.

Changing direction can be a useful ploy.

The very resistant horse rarely gives in without a fight. He tries a few more times to avoid the inevitable. We must therefore be prepared to use this procedure until he stops playing the game. Slowly, we find that fewer turns are needed and we can go more directly to where we want to be. Eventually, he stops resisting altogether and that's the end of it.

A helper can assist by driving from behind.

Driving from behind
Second on the list of tactics is driving from behind – on the assumption that I have a handy helper. I position myself at the head end, a little in front of the horse. This is to 'show by example' where I want him to go. As I walk forward (acting as leader, and showing by example) my handy helper comes up behind, waving and flapping her arms about.

The instinctive reaction of the horse is to move away from something coming up behind him, all the more if it's flapping about. Up goes his head, back go his ears and he starts moving.

Again, you keep up this routine until the horse goes freely forward of his own accord. How many times you have to repeat it depends on you, your helper and the horse. There is a knack to these things and, sometimes, it takes a bit of getting used to. If you haven't done it before, be prepared for some trial and error.

RUSHING WHEN LED
On the other side of the coin from refusing to go forwards is the horse who tries to pull away and rush off. Although the 'opposite' of refusing to go forwards, this is also an example of the horse not wanting to be led as we wish to lead him. Such a horse jiggles and pulls, and may throw his head about. The pace we are setting is too slow. He can't wait. Or maybe he just wants to get away.

From the horse's point of view, such a horse is wound up or over-excited. Most commonly, he is anxious to get back to his field. He is held in too tightly on the lead-rope and he doesn't like that either. Or maybe he's just annoyed and doesn't want to play the catching and leading game.

Dealing with the horse who rushes
Whatever the reason, I want such a horse to understand that he is not allowed to rush off, but I have to be subtle about it. Getting into a head-on battle of

FROM MY CASE BOOK

Among other problems, Ellie had a classic problem with leading. She wouldn't lead up the ramp and into a trailer. She would walk politely to the bottom of the ramp and just stand there, looking around for anything up to an hour or so. No amount of cajoling would persuade her go up the ramp. Any attempt to pull her up would (predictably) make her rear.

She was such a madam, was Ellie. She thought she could do whatever she liked – and if she didn't like it, she reared. With regard to loading, there was only one way to sort this mare out. Jess did the leading. I positioned myself so that, as she got to the foot of the ramp, I would be level with her rump. As her head-end got close to the ramp, I cracked a lunge whip loudly behind her. She shot up the ramp and into the trailer, without a second thought.

The next time, I positioned myself in the same place, just holding the lunge-whip a little raised and pointing towards her. She eyed it warily and then ran up the ramp. Terrific. Just what we wanted!

The next few times, I stood in the same place and had the lunge whip ready. We never needed to use the lunge whip again. The next step came by itself. I would just stand in the usual place and Ellie would trot up the ramp. Now, she just loads like a perfectly normal horse. She just walks calmly up the ramp and into the trailer. Now, either one of us can load her on our own.

wills only makes the horse fight harder. The trick is to bring him round in a circle. As he surges forward, I let him get about half a length ahead of me, then block his forward movement. All I have to do is take a firm hold of the lead-rope and pull it slightly backwards. The natural law of physics does the rest.

He starts turning in a circle around me. He can't help himself. He is already propelling himself forwards. The rope prevents him from continuing on the straight line, but he can't bring himself to stop. The urge to run is too strong. The anxiety or frustration produces a surge of energy. He needs to release it.

After a little while, having used up this surge of adrenalin-fired energy, the horse slows down and falls in line by himself. He knows he is restrained by the rope and can't go anywhere else, and also understands what he is supposed to be doing.

Dealing with a horse who rushes. Notice particularly, Jess's inner stillness and what she is doing with the rope. She is in no way flustered, but holds her ground and gives plenty of rope.

After a while, the horse has used up his adrenalin-fired energy and settles down.

If the horse starts surging forward again, you simply repeat the procedure. You put the message across in the most natural and easy way possible. At the same time, the need to express the sudden burst of energy is accommodated.

Peace is restored. The horse is happy. He's had his little tantrum and that's the end of it – or is it? As often as not, the horse will try again … and again, because learning is a process. It usually takes a few repetitions (Magic of Three!) for the message to sink in, but using the same 'tools' every time in the same calm, efficient workmanlike way, we get the result we want.

As often as not, problems with leading come from little more than lack of familiarity. The horse does not know us too well, and we don't know him. The routine he knew before has gone. He doesn't know quite what to expect.

This makes him anxious or nervous. As time goes by, he settles into his new routine and behaves himself. We have also shown him that we know how to take control of the situation and overcome his little resistances. He needs to know this too.

SUMMARY
❖ Allow the horse to find the position that suits him best.
❖ Following behind the leader is usually (but not always) the most comfortable position.
❖ Refusing to move should first be met with 'give and take' on the rope.
❖ Read the signs.
❖ Changing direction is the next port of call.
❖ As a last resort, drive from behind/give a smack on the rump.
❖ If he wants to rush away, make him circle round you.
❖ Stand your ground and let natural laws do the rest. Take control, not of the horse but of the situation.

17. WON'T TIE UP

This horse simply won't stand still. He fidgets, paws the ground, moves around and, in the worst case scenario, pulls back, breaks something and/or rears. The reason for this behaviour has to be diagnosed and responded to in an appropriate way.

FIDGETING

General agitation

From the horse's point of view, he is indicating that he is agitated. He would rather not be there. Where would he rather be? Back in his field – or anywhere else but here. Additionally, he is restrained by the headcollar, which gives him the feeling of entrapment. He doesn't like that either. It makes him feel helpless, and no horse, whether wild or domesticated, likes that.

Most commonly, such a horse has recently arrived in a new home. He feels insecure. He is not sure of what to expect and/or doesn't like the separation from his new-found friends and companions.

WHAT I WOULD DO

In this situation, I would simply ignore his behaviour and make the best of a bad job. The horse is agitated. Adrenalin is rising. He needs to move about, sniff the ground, look around and/or find things to nibble. Trying to make him stand still would only make the situation worse. It can be a little inconvenient, but nothing worse. In this way, I am also showing by example. There is nothing to worry about.

The essence here is acceptance and tolerance of the horse as he is. He's worried and, for whatever the reason, he is entitled to be.

As the horse moves around, I move with him, getting the job done as best I can. Slowly, the horse learns that nothing is achieved by this behaviour and that there is nothing to worry about. As his agitation subsides, his ability to stay still increases, until eventually he stops fidgeting altogether.

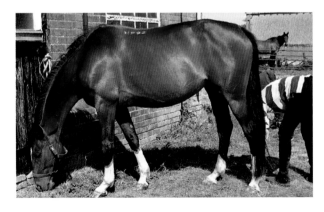

Simply ignore the fidgeting.

Underlying fear

On the other hand, rather than having a general feeling of agitation, it may be that the horse *does* have something to fear. He might be anxious because he knows what's coming next and he is not going to have an easy time of it. He's worried about it – and with justification. He knows he's going to be ridden and he doesn't like it. In this case, his dissatisfaction with riding must also be addressed, or he will be perpetually worried about it and no amount of tolerance will make the worry go away.

Fear of the saddle

Some horses get anxious and fidgety when the saddle appears, which may or may not be connected with anxiety about being ridden. What they mostly don't like is when the girth is yanked up so hard and tight that they are momentarily uncomfortable. It's rather like doing up your belt so tight that it makes you suck in your breath. If you had no control over it, it would be rather disconcerting. And so it is for the horse.

WHAT I WOULD DO

I would treat this horse as if he had never been saddled before. Holding the saddle (to let him know it's coming) I start by *gently* (but not too gently – I want him to feel it) patting and stroking along his back in the saddle area. I keep doing this until he is accepting and standing quietly. When the moment seems right, I raise the saddle up, taking care not to brush against his back with any part of it, and watch his reaction. If he shows signs of nervousness, I take the saddle down again and resume gentle patting and stroking.

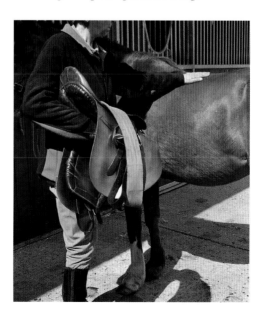

Saddling a fearful horse. Start by stroking the horse's back, and continue as shown overleaf.

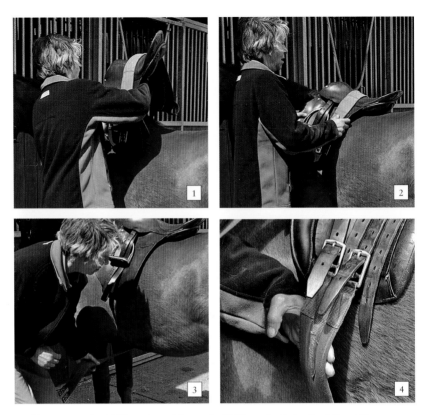

(1) Offer the saddle. (2) Place the saddle gently. (3) Move slowly to attach the girth. (4) Fasten girth gently, by increments.

However long it takes, I repeat this little procedure until I can place the saddle on his back without signs of anxiety or nervousness. Placing the saddle slightly up his withers, I then slide it back to the correct position to ensure that the hair underneath is not ruffled and is lying in the right direction.

In fastening the girth, I take care to move slowly and quietly as I reach down to bring it through. Again, I watch his reaction. If I notice any anxiety along the way, I stop and wait for him to relax before continuing.

Very gently, I do up the girth and take it up *only* as far as it goes without pulling or straining. It should be possible to slip a hand in very easily and show a little daylight.

In fact, I make a habit of doing up the girth like this with any horse, whether problematical or not. It seems only polite to let the horse get accustomed to this strap round his body before getting on and riding. For this reason, I always put the saddle on first, allowing the saddle to settle into place while I put on the bridle. All that remains is to check the girth before mounting and adjust if necessary. Horses often 'blow out' in anticipation of the girth being done up. This simple act of consideration means they don't have to bother!

PULLING BACK AND REARING

From the horse's point of view, if he is deeply upset, fidgeting may not be enough for him. He wants to escape. End of story! He may start by fidgeting, but with the objective of freeing himself. As this doesn't work, his anxiety rises. He pulls back, but this doesn't work either. If we are lucky, and his anxiety level is not too high, he respects the restraint and gives in to it. He also learns that there is no escape and that is more or less the end of it.

Commonly, though, he is startled. A sudden noise or rapid movement makes him jump. Wild-horse instinct kicks in, with the need to escape and run away. He pulls back violently and finds himself trapped. His fear now turns to the entrapment. He panics and struggles frantically. He may rear, or slip and fall to the ground. Either way, the original fear or provocation is forgotten. This horse is now terrified of being tied up.

If he hasn't already broken something, he must be released immediately. In the short term, this horse cannot be tied up again.

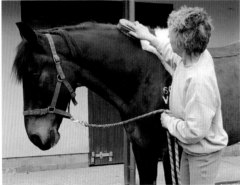

Top: Holding the lead-rope can by preferable to tying.
Above: Before long, the horse settles and becomes manageable.

WHAT I WOULD DO

Instead of tying up such a horse, I hold the rope and allow him the freedom to express his anxiety. At the same time, I keep him with me by allowing him to circle round me, if he wants to (see previous chapter). I keep the circle very small, which makes it uncomfortable for him, without actually preventing him from moving.

At first, his circling might be quite frantic and panicky, but he soon discovers that circling, quite literally, doesn't get him anywhere. Besides, the adrenalin rush is dying down. Nothing is more boring and tedious to the horse than going round in endless tight circles. Plus, it isn't easy. He isn't built for it.

Before long, he gets the message. Although he may still be fidgety and move about on the rope, he is manageable. Once again, I make the best of a bad job. In due course, he gives in completely and doesn't bother trying to get away. When the habit of standing still is well and truly established, I move towards tying him up again.

Ongoing remedy

If you adopt this initial procedure, I recommend, for the first few times, looping the rope, instead of tying it. This means that if the horse does pull back for any reason, he frees himself instantly, without meeting any resistance. Having achieved his objective, he won't go anywhere and the loose rope can be quickly and easily picked up. If this happens, revert to holding the rope for the duration of this session. It may mean that he isn't quite ready to be tied up and you must wait a little longer. Or it may just be an aberration and thus worth trying again. This, you must play by ear.

When I feel the time is right and the horse is fully accepting of staying where he is put, while I groom and tack up, I go back to tying up normally. However, I am always prepared for a relapse. The horse who has had a really bad time with tying up never forgets the experience. You never know when some little thing will trigger a relapse. If he does relapse, I simply go back to holding the rope for as long as it takes – usually only a day or two. Then I go through the looping procedure again, before tying up normally.

GROUND-TETHERING

It can be fun to teach your horse to ground-tether, particularly if he won't tie up. I discovered this by accident, with my first horse, Babe. I loved riding across the countryside, but there were quite a lot of farm gates, some of them constructed from wire, which were impossible to manage from the saddle. The easiest thing to do was dismount.

I would religiously take the reins over Babe's head, in case she got a bit impatient and wanted to move about, although she never did. She stood as solid as a rock and waited. Eventually, I got tired of holding the reins while fiddling about with various gate latches and wire. One day, I just dropped them to the ground. Still, she stood like a rock and waited patiently until I picked up the reins and led her forward. It got to the point where I could just throw the reins over her head, before even dismounting, and trust her implicitly to stay where she was. She never betrayed my trust.

Much the same principle can be used to train the horse to ground-tether – see photo sequence below.

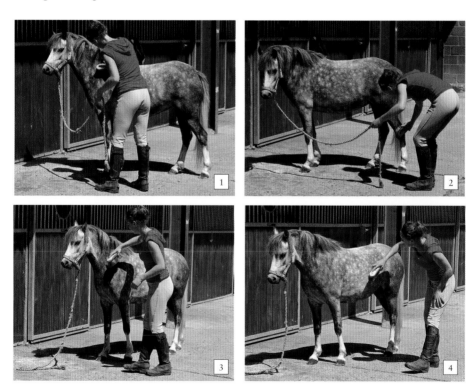

Ground-tethering. First, accustom the horse to grooming loose (i.e., not tied up). When he is totally happy with that, start by holding the horse and getting on with the job – see photos (1) and (2). Continue 'on the rope' until the moment feels right. Then let the rope drop to the ground (3). Notice the faint look of surprise on the mare's face, but a kindly word is spoken, so she goes back to sleep (4). You may also notice that not one of her feet has moved an inch – or even a millimetre. Each one trusts the other implicitly.

FROM MY CASE BOOK

Tequila was a demon to tie up. She broke anything that was breakable, including pulling tie-rings off walls. At shows, she could not be tied up to wait, like a normal horse. She had to be shut up in the horsebox. The root cause was a dislike of change that ran so deep it became a fear.

This was a horse who had only ever known a very secure and unchanging routine. Unfortunately for her, with us, change was a way of life in the early years. And so she was never tied up; I would hold the lead-rope. She would dance about a bit, then give in and stand quietly. She had once been very well trained. She knew what was expected, but fear got the better of her.

I guess it took a couple of years for her to learn that change of location was not the end of the world. Slowly but surely, she allowed herself to be tied up. However, if she showed any sign of agitation, I would revert to holding the rope again.

When she had settled to the idea of going to shows and competing, and no longer attempted to demolish the horsebox, she would be tied up normally, but always with a companion. If the companion went off to compete, I would take her too, leading her in hand and standing somewhere close by the ring and waiting.

Eventually, going to shows became no more of a trauma than her normal, everyday life. She could even go to a show on her own, be tied up with a hay-net and wait quietly like a normal horse.

SUMMARY

❖ Restraint from the headcollar makes the horse feel helpless.
❖ Accept him as he is.
❖ Make the best of a bad job and get on with it.
❖ Address other issues, such as problems with saddling and/or riding.
❖ When panic strikes, release him immediately.
❖ Restore confidence by allowing some freedom of movement.
❖ Reintroduce tying up normally by looping the rope first.
❖ Teach the horse to ground-tether. It's fun!

18. WON'T PICK UP HIS FEET

This is often a bone of contention. We have a tendency to assume that the horse will pick up his feet when asked. Why shouldn't he? It's easy enough, isn't it? He can stand on three. Yes, he can, but the question is – what does it mean to him?

WHY THE HORSE OBJECTS

From the horse's point of view, his feet (and legs) are perhaps his most precious commodity. They are the front line of his defence. Run first, ask questions afterwards. If he can't run away, he feels trapped and helpless. The wild horse would only ever lift one foot for a moment, usually to scratch himself, or get rid of a fly. He would never hold it up for any length of time. This is why he finds holding any of his feet up for us to pick them out or put shoes on so difficult.

A foal's response to having his leg held.

Look at the reaction of the foal in the photo when a hand simply closes round his lower leg. His first (wild-horse) instinct is to free himself. He lifts up his leg, in the hope that whatever is holding it will loosen. His ears show that he is a little puzzled by this strange turn of events – but he is not yet frightened. If the hold were maintained, he would panic and fight. It wasn't: his leg was released a moment or two later. The incident was quickly forgotten, although the first seed of the idea that he should pick up his feet when asked was planted in his head.

Thus we learn that the horse must be trained to pick up his feet with as much care and attention as any other part of his training. If not properly trained, his immediate response is the fight and flight reflex. Equally, if the task is mishandled in any way he reverts to his instinct, which is to pull his foot away.

Patting the rump indicates good intentions.

TRAINING

Whether or not he was trained before, I would put such a horse through the same basic training, reading the signs and using the 'stop and wait' technique. I start by standing next to his shoulder, to show that I have no fear. I give him a couple of firm pats on the neck if I don't know the horse, or on the shoulder if I do. At the back end, I do the same on his rump. Doing this shows my good intentions and serves as a kind of warning. I check to make sure there is no flinching. If he does flinch, I stop and wait, stay where I am, talk to him, keep my hand still and wait until the flinching stops.

The first stage

The first achievable target is, as usual, determined by the horse's response. I want to get down as far as the horse will allow me to go. I start sliding my hand down his shoulder onto his upper leg, patting at first as I go. As I get about halfway down his upper leg, I stop patting and simply slide my hand downwards in a firm and confident manner. I want the horse to feel my touch, but not be upset by it. My hand movement is steady and assured, neither too fast nor too slow. It isn't only about *what* we do, but the way we do it.

Starting down the leg.

The speed of descent depends on the horse. If he is very nervous, I go carefully, maybe patting as I go. If he is confident to this point (i.e. standing still and quiet) I keep the hand pressure even and proceed to the top of his leg. If, at this point, he flinches, I keep the hand in place, with much the same pressure and stop, holding my hand where it is, and wait for him to relax.

Reading the signs

It is usually around the knee (or hock, on the hind leg) that a horse starts to show the first sign of agitation. The head goes up. He looks anxious, or he

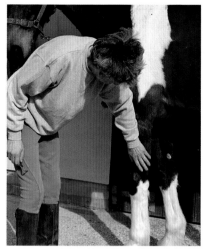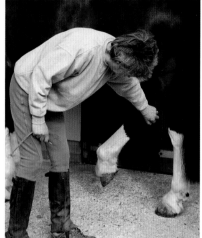

Making progress: stop if the horse seems anxious.

just starts to wriggle. When this happens, I stop and wait. I have got to the edge of his comfort zone. I keep my hand where it is, maintaining the same constant pressure. I stay very still and wait until he thinks to himself, 'This is OK: there is no harm in it' and relaxes.

He has nothing to worry about. This is where I want him.

The second stage

The next step is to move the boundary further down. I slide my hand down a little further, with the same slow but calm confidence. I want him to be reassured by my touch, not tickled by it. At the first sign of anxiety, I keep my hand where it is, maintain the same pressure, and stop and wait.

When he relaxes, I wait for another moment or two, then move on down a bit more. It is important to maintain the hand pressure on his leg. It must be neither too strong, nor too soft. Horses like a firm touch: they don't like to be either gripped or tickled.

Timing

When you do this, timing is of the essence. You must not move on down his leg until he is fully relaxed and accepting of your hand where it is. If you move on too soon, his agitation rises and you are back to square one. At the same time, try to keep your progress flowing down his leg. When he has relaxed under your hand and been given a moment, move on.

Show no fear

Even if you feel slightly nervous when doing this, you must mask it. This is easier than it sounds. You tell yourself to act, or behave as if you have no fear. That's all there is to it. Horses are highly susceptible to any fear or nervousness in us. They pick it up in a flash. As soon as they get the faintest whiff of fear or nervousness, the wild-horse herd instinct comes into play and they are nervous too.

The third stage

When the horse is relaxed and not showing any sign of distress, I will move on down towards his knee (or hock, on the hind leg). It is here that he may start to get worried and move away a bit. I stay calmly with it, keeping my hand in place, as before. The essence is that I stay calm, firm and completely in control.

Slowly but surely, stopping and waiting at the right moment, I get down to the fetlock. This is where the real trouble is likely to start, but I maintain my composure and carry on as before. If the horse snatches his foot away, I wait for him to put it back down and start again, a little higher up the leg. In other words, I go back a step or two, to restore his trust and confidence. I want him to lift his foot when I ask, not when he feels like it.

It is here, in particular, that the handler must show no fear. If you go nervously towards his foot, jumping away as soon as he flinches, he says to himself, 'Well, I'm not having that then.' Any trust and confidence you have achieved so far goes straight out of the window. If he does anything other than keep his foot on the ground, you must stay with it. He needs to know that you are in control.

Finally, we come to the tricky bit, which is the lift. Here, one of three things will happen. He may plant the foot and refuse point-blank to move it, or he will lift it so fast that we are caught by surprise, then try to snatch it away by rapidly moving his leg backwards and forwards. If we are lucky, he will lift his foot obligingly, but wriggle a bit.

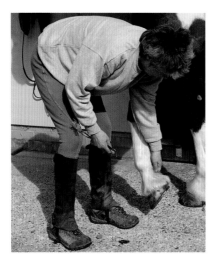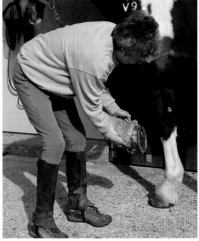

Getting the horse to bend at the knee is the key to him lifting his foot.

When he plants his foot, there is no choice but to insist that he MUST do as we ask. If he has hair on his fetlock (feathers) I grasp it firmly and pull, more in a backward direction than upward. If he has no hair, I grasp him firmly round the pastern in a fairly tight grip. The aim is to break the lock he has on his leg and make him bend at the knee. Once the foot is off the ground, I place the other hand underneath it, to hold it there. Now, I am home and dry!

On the foreleg, you can physically pull the leg forwards, just above the knee, quickly repositioning yourself once the lift is achieved. With the hind leg, you can only work at loosening his grip by pulling the foot backwards. A useful ploy is to lean your bodyweight heavily against his rump. (This can also be done on the shoulder.) He is slightly unbalanced and your job is made that much easier. Whichever way you do it, YOU MUST PREVAIL!

The worst-case scenario is when he whips his foot off the ground and starts throwing it about, mostly in a backwards and forwards movement. From his point of view, his foot is trapped. He is simply trying to free it and this is the only way he knows to do it. It is often thought that he trying to kick, but this is not the case. If he wanted to kick, he would swing his rump round, so he could get a backward swing at you.

Unfortunately for the horse, the only way through his fear at this point is for the handler to hang on. I take a step sideways, so I am out of harm's way, and continue with 'stop and wait'. It is quite hard and requires some strength, but is not as hard as it seems. Swinging his foot about like that means the horse is actually in a weakened position. As he only has three feet on the ground, he is unbalanced – and he knows it.

Watch any competent farrier and you see that this is exactly what he does. If you can't do it yourself, find someone who can. This is the only way the horse will ever learn that he can't get away with this resistance.

In this way, I work my way round all four feet. Each foot must be treated separately and worked on individually. Each session should include work on all four feet – where appropriate. It is also a good idea to vary the order, so the horse does not learn to anticipate. Many an owner comes unstuck because the horse will only lift his feet in a specific order. This can be a real nuisance if we only want to lift one particular foot to inspect it for any reason,

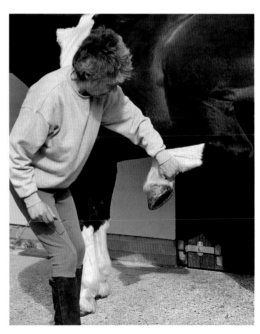

If the horse starts throwing his leg around, step to the side and hang on.

such as to check for a stone or other cause of lameness. Certainly, there are times when we want a horse to lift just one foot, without going round all the others first.

As is usually the case, complete transformation is not instantaneous. The next few times we go to lift his feet, we continue with the careful 'stop and wait' approach. What we find, as time goes by, is that there is less stopping and waiting. We can slide our hands smoothly down his leg and he obligingly picks up his feet.

> **EXPERT TIP**
> Always start the foot-lifting process by placing a hand on the horse's shoulder or rump, giving a couple of friendly pats or slaps and going on down his leg from there. This gives the horse warning and prepares him for what is to come.

SUMMARY
- ❖ Training to lift feet must be done with as much care and attention as any other training.
- ❖ Use the 'stop and wait' technique.
- ❖ Show no fear.
- ❖ Read the signs.
- ❖ Start high up, where the horse is comfortable.
- ❖ Be firm and confident in your manner.
- ❖ Stop at the first sign of agitation; move on when the horse is ready.
- ❖ The speed of descent depends on the horse.
- ❖ Timing is of the essence.
- ❖ At the point of lift, you must prevail.
- ❖ If you can't manage the lift, find someone who can.

19. THE HEAD-SHY/ EAR-SHY HORSE

Somewhere along the line, the head/ear-shy horse has been mistreated about the head. It doesn't take much: too much fumbling around is enough for the horse to say, 'Leave my head alone.' Luckily for him, he has the perfect defence mechanism. He can throw his head around all over the place, until we either find the way to make peace or give up.

FINDING SOLUTIONS

Freedom and Bribery

Most head-shy horses are friendly enough – until you go near their head. Nonetheless, I will start by showing that I am a good person to know. My peace-offering will also be used as the substance of the bribery that will both reward and encourage the horse to stay with me. I use pony nuts or similar as they are small, dry and not too sweet. For this work, I fill a bum-bag so I have access to a constant supply.

As trust is very much part of the picture, I do not tie the horse up, hold or restrain him in any way while I am working. I want him to stay with me of his own free will. Also, if I make an error of judgement and he has a bad reaction, I don't want him to feel trapped as this will only reinforce his fear.

NB: *If putting the headcollar on is part of the problem, this work can be done with the horse loose in a pen or stable.*

Accept what you can get

Having shown that I am a good person to know and judging that the horse is relaxed, I start by feeding some more treats and simultaneously laying my free hand somewhere on his neck. I watch his reaction carefully. As with picking up feet, we always begin at a point where the horse is comfortable. Thus we start from a place of trust

Top: Offering pony nuts is a good start.
Above: If the horse seems relaxed, try laying your free hand on his neck.

and confidence, which is, if you like, the first building block. The objective is to strengthen, then build on it. Right at the beginning, with the horse in the photo, I find I can get my hand quite near his head, so this is where I start, feeding treats to make it a very pleasant experience.

Stop and wait
Before moving my hand any further up his neck, I hold it where it is, while I replenish the pony nut supply in my hand. I do not make another move, until he is happily accepting the treats. Thus, his mind is partially taken away from what

my hand is doing. Watching the horse's body language for the first flicker of fear or distrust, I must always continue to gauge whether it is prudent to ask for a little more, or call it a day. If the horse is pushed too far or too fast, confidence is lost and we have to start all over again.

Moving on
Having gained trust and confidence so far, and still rubbing, I move carefully towards the horse's ear. The moves are incremental, a little bit at a time. All the while I am watching the horse's reaction. If a horse is still accepting of my touch, I progress a little bit further. My goal is for the horse's calm acceptance of my hand rubbing all over the head, ears and face.

Top: Offer more treats and watch for reactions.
Above: Work towards the ear in small increments.

At the first sign of resistance, which will be a flick of the head either up or away, I stop and wait for the horse to relax. I know that I have reached the edge of the horse's current comfort zone. Keeping the treats coming, I either stay where I am until the horse relaxes or back up a little and go back to where he was comfortable and work my way forward again. Work like this depends on intuition and judgement of the individual horse.

Taking time
With a seriously head-shy horse, I will spend about fifteen minutes per day getting as far as I can go – which may not be very far. Above all, I want to maintain trust and confidence. It may take a couple of days to work up to the head and/or ears. If this is the case, so be it.

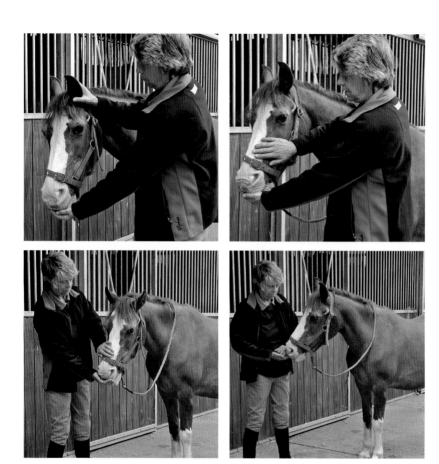

Top left: Touching the ears may require time and patience.
Top right: Work gently around the face and head, watching for 'stop and wait' moments.
Bottom left: Progress to work from both sides.
Bottom right: It is a good sign when the horse takes more notice of the treats than the handling.

The ears are usually tricky. At first, I simply lay my hand around the base and wait for acceptance. As long as the touch is light, the treats win him over. If, however, he shows too much agitation, I move my hand back towards his neck and start again. Having done nothing to cause real distress and shown my understanding, we get there sooner or later.

Having established the principle of the way we are working, I simply work my way round the various parts of his head and face until he is comfortable with my touching, stroking and rubbing anywhere. Notice in the top right photo the uncertainty, with one ear forward and the other back. This is a 'stop and wait' moment and an area that might need a little more attention.

From here on, I follow the horse, working my way around as seems appropriate at the time. Along the way, I also work both sides, usually alternating on a daily basis. I want him to be comfortable whichever side he is approached from.

The treats are very tasty. Before too long, he has understood where they are coming from and is looking for them. I take this as a good sign. I now know that his interest in the reward is greater than his fear. Nonetheless, I must still proceed with caution. His trust is very delicately balanced.

There may be a moment when the horse is distracted and turns his head away. I go with the flow, replenish the treats in my hand and wait for his attention to come back to me, at which point we pick up where we left off.

Moving away from bribery

At this point, there is still some way to go. Does the horse trust me enough to allow me to touch his sensitive places without the use of bribery? This can only be assessed by judgement, but as long as there has been some continual improvement/progress, I can be fairly sure that I can safely move on.

The next session starts with what the horse knows. I produce pony nuts as I did before and do some general stroking and caressing. When the time feels right, I go right back to the beginning but without the use of bribery.

I lay one hand on his upper neck, gently caressing, and then start gently rubbing and caressing all over his upper neck, head and face and following much the same procedure as before.

By now, I am reasonably confident but watching all the while for any adverse reaction. When I can get to a head-hug at the end without the horse flinching or pulling away, I reckon the job is just about done.

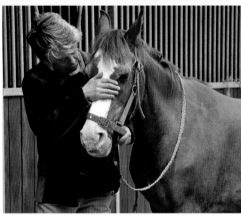

Top: If the horse is distracted, go with the flow.
Middle: In due course, move towards stroking without the use of bribery.
Bottom: Once it is possible to hug the horse's head without resistance, the job is done.

FROM MY CASE BOOK

Rosa, a 15hh Thoroughbred, was the most head-shy horse I have ever met. Just getting a headcollar on was struggle, never mind a bridle. And yet, she was the sweetest horse you could ever hope to find, so kind and gentle – until you went near her head. Then, she was blatantly terrified.

From what her owner told me, she was raised as every horse should be raised, running free with a few other mares and foals, and very little human interference. This would certainly explain her exceptionally gentle nature. Her first rider, so I was told, was a young girl of twelve – which also says a lot about how she was raised and her training. All she had ever known was people who were not only kind and gentle, but also knew how to relate to horses.

As a seven-year-old, Rosa went out on loan and came back a year later, a different horse. No one could touch her anywhere round her head. Just getting a headcollar on was a bit of a battle. Bringing her back to normal was going to be quite a challenge.

It took about three weeks of working with her almost every day. From time to time, when it felt right and we had made good progress, she had a day or two off to go away and think about it. It's called 'latent learning' and does any training process the world of good.

As she was so incredibly sensitive round the mouth, when I got to bridling, I started with a hackamore, partly so we could carry on riding her, but also so she could get completely comfortable with the whole bridling process.

It took about a year to move from a hackamore to a normal bitted bridle but she wasn't ridden that much. This process could probably have been done in three to six months had there been a reason to ride more often. It's all about habituation, which should only be done in the context in which it is needed.

Rosa is one of the most rewarding horses I ever worked with. At the outset, she looked like mission impossible but she came right back to normal. By the end of it, you would never have known she had a problem in the first place. But woe betide anyone who got even slightly rough around her head. That underlying fear never went away.

SUMMARY

The head-shy horse must be de-sensitised. The basic principles are:

❖ Freedom and bribery.
❖ Accept what you can get.
❖ Stop and wait.
❖ Extend the boundaries very slowly and carefully.
❖ Break the process down into the smallest possible parts.
❖ Work both sides.
❖ Complete acceptance of touching/handling round the head comes before bridling.

20. WON'T ACCEPT THE BIT OR BRIDLE

When the horse meets a bridle for the first time in his life it comes as no great surprise, except for the bit. He has got used to things being attached to his head, but this thing inside his mouth is something else.

WHY THE HORSE OBJECTS

From the horse's point of view, he can't understand it. What is this strange thing in his mouth? It is not good to eat and it won't go away. He doesn't like it and spends some time trying to eject it. He opens his mouth wide and tries to drop the bit or push it out with his tongue. He flings his head about and tries to shake it out. We call this 'mouthing'. In the adjacent photos you can see by his ears that Dibley, bridled for the first time, looks rather puzzled: 'What is this thing in my mouth? Why can't I make it go away?'

Wearing a bridle for the first time is, as a minimum, a puzzle for the horse.

Within about five or ten minutes, he learns that it doesn't go away until the bridle is taken off. He learns to accept both bit and bridle and stops even trying to get rid of the bit. On the whole, he discovers there is no harm to it and, besides, he has no choice. He finds that out very early on.

The second element to the bridling procedure is that we must fiddle, not only with his head and ears, which is bad enough, but also with his very sensitive mouth. Most horses don't like having their mouths held open. This is because a horse's mouth is as precious to him as his feet. His mouth is crucial to his survival. It is also equipped with a lot of nerve endings, which are needed to guide him in what he eats.

The whole bridling procedure, therefore, needs to be done as efficiently as possible – and this is where problems with bridling usually start. There is too much fumbling around for his liking.

Unfortunately, there are also people who try to make the horse keep his head still by holding on to an ear. Evidently, the horse likes this even less than the bit or bridle. He soon learns to associate bridling with pain and discomfort and quickly becomes head- and/or ear-shy (see Chapter 19). He now doesn't want anyone to go anywhere near his head or ears for any reason.

TEACHING ACCEPTANCE

I usually start by getting the clutter out of the way, taking the headcollar off the horse's head and fastening it round his neck. He knows he is still tied up and can't get away. There is nothing worse than getting hooked up on the headcollar at a moment when you need to be sliding the bridle smoothly upward.

I want the process to be as smooth and easy as I can make it. I will also break the process down into the smallest possible stages. There is no hurry; I can take my time. Horses gain confidence from 'slow and easy'.

Start by fastening the headcollar round the horse's neck.

Presenting the bridle

The first stage is to present the bridle and watch his reaction to it. If he is OK about it, I move in a little closer and take hold of his nose. This lets him know that the process is about to begin and also helps to keep his head in the right place.

By this action, I also show that I am in control. If he wriggles, or tries to pull his head away, I 'stop and wait' (keeping my hand in the same position on his nose) until he is calm and still.

My normal routine for bridling is first to put the reins over the horse's head. I start as I mean to go on. If he moves his head about, I slow down. Everything I do is gauged by the horse's reaction.

Now comes the first tricky bit, which is approaching the bridle to his head. This is where he is most likely to really start resisting. If he moves his head away, I keep my hands where they are, rest my upper hand against his forehead and maintain this position until he stops moving.

I become the follower. Wherever his head goes, my hands go too, almost as if they are glued or fixed to him. As long as I stay quiet and maintain my inner stillness, the horse soon gives in. Nothing bad is happening and he really doesn't want to be flinging his head about. There is too much effort involved. Before long, he understands that nothing bad is happening. So far, so good! He can cope with that.

But now the horse knows what is coming. He starts to get agitated. Following as before, with my arm still resting on his forehead, I stay with him and approach the bit to his mouth.

Top: Put the reins over the horse's head.
Above: Fitting the bridle is when the horse may start resisting – become a follower to any movements.

Opening the mouth

Next comes the really tricky bit, which is politely asking him to open his mouth. Politeness is essential. Most problems start by either trying to force the bit into his mouth, or assuming that he will just take it.

Hold the bit across the palm of your hand, with your hand spread open.

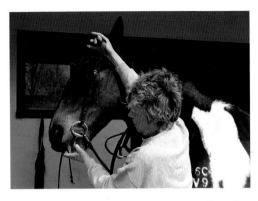

Getting the horse to open his mouth may require polite firmness, but avoid force.

Next, insert your thumb between his lips. Be quite firm about this and don't worry, he won't bite. A bite is only considered and done with the front teeth. An intrusion into the side of the mouth is either to be ejected or avoided. By opening his mouth, he thinks he may succeed in ejecting the intrusion. He isn't entirely wrong!

He may be resistant and refuse. He may also, once again, try to move his head away. If he does, simply follow him again, keeping your hands in place and physically pull your hand and thumb downwards. The quicker this is over and done with, the better.

HORSE FACT

More often than not, the assumption that a horse will take the bit automatically is a false one. Some horses will open their mouths as soon as the bit is presented, but they are few and far between. Most need to be asked and we must always assume that they need to be asked unless or until we find out differently. This reluctance to open the mouth voluntarily is the last bastion of his choice – and he is entitled to it.

If you're not sure how to do it, practise asking him to open his mouth without the threat of the bridle present. There is a knack to it. It can be done any time, anywhere, with just a headcollar on. Or practise on another, more obliging horse.

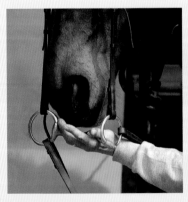 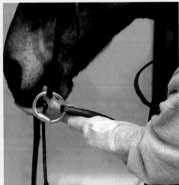

Presenting the bit to the horse's mouth.

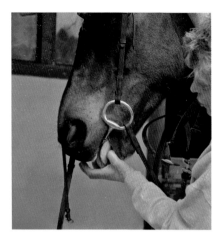
Sliding in the bit.

If he is very resistant and refuses to open his mouth, it is permissible to insert thumb and little finger over his gums and pull downward with the 'give and take' technique. As his head goes up, you pull down. As his head comes down, you release the pressure … and so on, until he gets the message and opens his mouth.

When – and only when – his mouth is open, pull the head-piece upward and slide the bit smoothly into his mouth. Once it is in there, the worst is over and the bridling process is completed normally.

The resistant horse may take a while to return to normal. As usual, he is quick to learn bad habits and slow to let go of them, but the calmer and more efficient you make the whole process, the quicker he will stop fussing about it. Simply continue with the 'stop and wait' procedure and opening his mouth correctly each time you put the bridle on.

The mouth-shy horse

Too much fumbling and/or rough handling can make a horse toss his head in all directions to avoid letting you go near his mouth. Milly, the mare in the photo, isn't head-shy in the true sense of the word. She is mouth-shy and needs de-sensitising.

WHAT I WOULD DO

I do this in much the same way as de-sensitising a head-shy horse. Starting higher up the head, where the horse is comfortable, I work my way down towards the mouth with a gentle, circular, rubbing movement. Although holding the headcollar, I do so lightly. If Milly suddenly pulls her head away, I don't want to add to her distress by restraining her.

Over a few days, I slowly, carefully work around the nose and mouth of a mouth-shy horse until he is comfortable and accepting of my touch. From there, it is only one

Too much fumbling and rough handling can make a horse mouth-shy.

It pays dividends to work carefully around the nose and mouth of a mouth-shy horse.

small step to get to asking him to open his mouth normally. Not being used to it and with a history of resistance, he may be a little unwilling at first. By stopping and waiting at appropriate moments and with gentle perseverance, the horse soon gives in.

If you have such a horse and want to carry on riding while you are resolving this issue, use a hackamore. This has the added benefit of helping the horse to understand that he can be bridled without a fuss.

A hackamore can be useful on a mouth-shy horse.

THE HORSE WHO WON'T DROP THE BIT

Occasionally, I come across a horse with the opposite problem to that addressed so far. He won't let go of the bit when the time comes to take the bridle off. Originally, he probably threw his head up and the bit banged his teeth. He didn't like that. Throwing up his head and hanging on to the bit soon became a habit.

There are two ways to proceed here. The first is to take hold of the head-piece in the usual way, stop and wait until he stops throwing his head about, then proceed normally. It is often the action of lifting the bridle to get it over his ears that starts the resistance. The horse feels that slight increase of pressure on the bit and away he goes. If possible then, take the bridle over his ears and hold it there, before stopping and waiting.

If this is too difficult, instead of trying to take the bridle off normally, undo one or both cheek-pieces and let the bit fall out of his mouth. Then take the rest of the bridle off normally. Again, you may have to use 'stop and wait' to get the rest off, but that's OK. He will get the idea eventually.

SUMMARY
- ❖ Make the process easy.
- ❖ Break the process down into the smallest possible parts.
- ❖ Get the clutter out of the way.
- ❖ Impart confidence by being slow and easy.
- ❖ Give warning that the process is about to begin.
- ❖ If the horse moves his head, go quietly into 'follower' mode.
- ❖ Ask politely for him to open his mouth.
- ❖ Only insert the bit when the mouth is open.
- ❖ A bitless bridle is recommended for some time afterwards.
- ❖ A normal bit can be introduced at a much later date.
- ❖ If he won't drop the bit (when taking the bridle off) use 'stop and wait' or undo the cheek-pieces.

21. WON'T STAND STILL FOR MOUNTING

We have learned that it is not natural for the horse to stand still, unless he chooses to do so, or is restrained. Like a few other things we tend to take for granted, he must be trained to stand still for our convenience. Some horses are not trained at all. Others 'forget' through mishandling.

WHY THE HORSE WON'T STAND STILL

From the horse's point of view, standing still and waiting while we climb on board makes no sense at all. He knows that as soon as we are in the saddle, he will be asked to go, so what are we waiting for?

He has no concept of how setting off before we are ready might be inconvenient. He is not bothered that we might not be sitting comfortably, with our feet safely in the stirrups. His only concern is to answer to his instincts and get on with it. Where we come unstuck is making an issue out of it and trying to force what does not come naturally. Most problems with mounting arise through trying to make the horse stand still when he instinctively wants to do otherwise.

Professional riders overcome this little characteristic by allowing the horse to walk away while they are mounting. It isn't so difficult when you get used to it and keeps the horse relaxed and comfortable with very little effort. Notice the long, loose rein in the photo and how there is no attempt made to control the horse in any way. Once mounted, the rider picks up the reins and sorts everything out. The horse understands this little procedure and it all works perfectly well.

Professional riders often don't bother to make the horse stand still for mounting.

TEACHING THE HORSE TO STAND

Whether the horse has 'forgotten' his training, or was never trained in the first place, I would put him through the same training procedure. I break the process down into the smallest possible parts and use the 'stop and wait' technique. Each step or stage becomes an achievable target.

EXPERT TIP

You are out hacking and you need to dismount. Your horse tries to rush off when you want to get back on again. A handy tip is to face him in the direction he *doesn't* want to go – usually away from home. That quickly puts an end to his desire to go forward.

Work in stages

Stage 1

The first stage is to get the horse standing where I want him. If possible, I face him up to a substantial fence or gate. His instinctive reaction is usually to move off in a forward direction. A fence or gate acts as a natural barrier. Alternatively, I face him in a direction in which he doesn't want to go. That would be facing away from the yard and/or his field-mates. This is because his natural inclination is not to move any further away from his source of comfort and security.

Moving to the mounting position, I take one rein in each hand. I may need to prevent the horse from turning away (which would be a natural reaction) and with one rein in each hand I can do this very easily.

Beginning the mounting process: if the horse moves his feet, start again.

When I am satisfied – and not before – that the horse has understood what is wanted so far, I put my reins into one hand and raise my foot towards the stirrup. If he moves, even a tiny step sideways, I bring my foot back down to the ground, re-position the horse and start again. If he moves his head, that's OK – It's his feet that must stay planted.

Stage 2

The next step is to put weight on the stirrup but without actually rising up. If he moves, I come back down, re-position if necessary, go back to the beginning and start all over again. He MUST be standing of his own free will, i.e., NOT held by the reins.

Stage 3

The next step is to raise myself up and stand on the stirrup. As before, if he moves his feet, I come back down, re-position and start again.

Stage 4

Finally, we come to the full mount. Even as I swing my leg over his back, I am prepared to come back down again and start again. The horse must understand that no movement is allowed until I ask him to do so. Eventually, he does understand that this is a standing still exercise.

Notes on the process

Two things are of paramount importance to this process. The first is that the horse is NOT restrained on the reins, but is standing still of his own free will. During 'work in progress' they must be loose. There must be no pressure on the bit whatsoever.

Second, as soon as the horse moves, no matter which stage you are at, you stop where you are and go back to the beginning. Even if you are almost there and swinging the right leg over, you must get down and go back to the beginning. This is the only way he will learn that he must stand still for the whole process.

Top: Putting weight in the stirrup without rising.
Middle and bottom: Standing in the stirrup – if the horse moves his feet, start again.

The mounted horse should be taught to remain stationary until the reins are picked up.

Once mounted

Once mounted, it is useful to teach the horse that the signal to move on is when you pick up the reins. As long as they are loose, he stays where he is.

Having achieved the full mount, that is enough for the day. I do not recommend repeating the procedure until the next time you want to ride. As it goes against his instincts, this is a hard lesson for a horse to learn. If you try to repeat the exercise, he will get fed up, be ever less inclined to cooperate, and his behaviour will get worse.

If, on the other hand, you go through the procedure whenever you ride, it makes more sense to the horse as you put it into context. He comes to understand that this is what is wanted before you ride. As long as you go patiently through the same procedure each time, after three, or maybe four, repetitions he'll get it. What you find is that you simply come back down less and less until you can mount normally without having to hold on to your horse.

As a general rule, if handled correctly, most horses can master this basic training in one session of fifteen to twenty minutes. A few, however, are more difficult and may need two or three sessions. Each session is based on how far the horse is willing to go. In other words, you stop when it all seems too difficult for him.

Subsequently, use the same procedure every time you mount, stopping if he moves and quietly going back to the beginning. By the third or fourth time, the lesson should be assimilated and stopping and waiting are no longer needed. However, should he relapse into his former behaviour, you simply return to the training procedure.

Above all, this is about acceptance and patience. If the horse does not instantly do what you want, you accept it. This is the way he is right now. Patiently, you deal with it – as many times as it takes, but always keeping the horse on track and moving his training forward. There must always be progress, no matter how small the improvement. Your efforts are in vain if there is none.

Assisted training

If you have someone to help you, there is an easier route. Your goal is the same. You want the horse to stand still while you mount *without any restraint*. He must simply learn what to do without your holding on to him in any way – so it's a loose rein throughout.

Ask your handy helper to stand in front of your horse to physically block the way forward and *lightly* hold the bit-rings to *suggest* to the horse that he stays where he is. (The signals are so clear they usually get the idea without any difficulty.) If any control is needed on the bit, usually to prevent the horse from turning away, it should be no more than a very light touch.

Repeat the procedure each time you mount but with the following progression in mind. When the time is right, usually on the second or third attempt, your helper simply stands in front of the horse and does nothing. Now, the physical block is enough to remind the horse what to do. Over time, your helper stands ever further back until no longer needed. Job done!

If your horse is very fidgety and resistant to standing still, use bribery. Your helper stands directly in front of the horse as before and drip-feeds little treats. As the supply keeps coming, a little at a time, it's not long before the horse is more interested in when, and from where, the next lot is coming than in what you are doing – as you can see in the adjacent photo from Pudsie's interest in what my hands are doing.

You then follow the same procedure. As the horse gets the message and understands what is wanted, the treats are slowly withdrawn. Once again, your helper just stands directly in front of the horse and progressively moves further back until they are not needed any more.

The essence of this method is the timing. When to move on by standing

Top: The helper stands in front of the horse, holding the bit-rings lightly.
Above: Bribery may be useful on a fidgety horse.

back and/or slowing down and then withdrawing the delivery of treats has to be judged according to the individual horse. Your helper therefore needs to be sensitive to progress. It's no good just shovelling food at his face and expecting it to work. All you will establish is an enduring habit and the need for a helper every time you mount.

HORSE FACT
Standing still for mounting is intrinsically so difficult for the horse that most professional riders don't make an issue out of it. Making no attempt to restrain him, they simply get on while the horse is moving forwards, almost invariably, in a steady, quiet walk. Once you get used to it, this really isn't so difficult and it does make life that little bit easier for the horse.

SUMMARY
❖ Standing still for mounting goes against the horse's natural instincts.
❖ He must be trained (or retrained) to stand still.
❖ Break the process down into the smallest possible parts.
❖ Use the 'stop and wait' technique.
❖ Don't move on until you are satisfied.
❖ He must learn that he is not allowed to move until told to do so.
❖ He must be standing still of his own free will.
❖ Keep using the same procedure until the bad habit is broken.

22. AGGRESSION: KICKING AND BITING

As a general rule, wild horses don't have much use for aggression, and our own are no different. All horses prefer peace and harmony. In the wild, the natural purpose of aggressive behaviour is to educate the young (although usually only with threat gestures rather than actual kicks or bites), see off intruders or defend themselves against predators.

PROVOCATION AND REACTION

It is only our intervention that brings out aggressive behaviour in our horses. We subject them to things that don't come naturally and then expect them to put up with it. Of course, mostly they do. Learning to accept what we want without demur is an integral part of their training.

However, as a result of mishandling somewhere along the way, some horses develop aggressive tendencies which are essentially defence mechanisms. In the adjacent photo, Ellie is blatantly saying, 'Leave me alone. I don't like what you're doing to me!' (*Notice Jess's inner stillness as she puts herself out of reach of a flying hind foot and just gets on with the job. Ellie can be ticklish just there and often displays irritation or temper.*)

A feature of the wild-horse herd is the unity of the group. They are essentially a family group. Our own horses take on the same characteristics. Strangers are viewed with suspicion and, if they get too close, may be driven away.

Horses may use aggressive responses to indicate dislike of various types of handling.

Strangers may be driven away.

This is why we often see aggressive behaviour when a new horse is introduced to the group. As long as they all have plenty of space, so that the newcomer has room to keep a safe distance until he is accepted, no harm comes from these encounters. Wild-horse instinct comes into play as the newcomer understands immediately that he has been relegated to the bottom of the pecking order and must work his way slowly and carefully into the group.

From the horse's point of view, kicking and biting are warnings. The message is: 'Get out of my space. You're too close. Leave me alone.' In their own company, horses know what it means and respond accordingly. No horse ever argues with one who is threatening to kick or bite, and even less with one who makes contact. The respect is instant.

When a horse turns his aggression onto us, something is seriously wrong. The message is the same: 'Leave me alone. Get out of my space. Go away.' The question we must ask is – why? We are the essence of love and kindness. We shower him with affection. Why does he want us to leave him alone, get out of his space or go away? As usual, there are several answers, but one thing we know for sure. He is deeply disturbed about it.

What disturbs him most is when we persist. According to his equine code of conduct, we should respect his feelings and do what he says – but we don't. We carry on and fuss about, invading his space and trying to make the best of it. At the same time, we worry that we might get hurt, so our movement tends

Leave me alone!

to be timid, or sharp and defensive. The horse likes this even less. He is annoyed enough already, but our efforts to avoid flying hooves or teeth are even more disturbing. And indeed sometimes, we do get hurt as we carry on regardless.

UNDERSTANDING THE MESSAGE

It might be said that the purpose of a horse's aggression towards us is to educate us – and in a sense, this is true. When he flattens his ears, nips, bites or kicks, he is behaving as if we are another horse who needs to learn a lesson or two. There is something he wants us to know. And we have to work out what he is trying to tell us.

Broadly, the message is always the same. He is angry. Something about us is making him angry. What could it be? Let's look for a minute at what horses like and dislike.

Horses like:	Horses dislike:
• The calm of inner stillness. • Gentle, but also competent handling. • Slow, easy movement and a firmly confident touch. • Friendliness. • Above all, they like to feel they are in safe hands.	• Brisk efficiency, when it borders on being hurried and careless. • Inefficiency. • Soft and soppy handling. • Over-indulgence. • Over-confidence. • Persistence at the wrong time and place • Timidity and nervousness. • Rapid movement. • Feeling pursued, chased or trapped.

To reiterate, the purpose of an adult horse reprimanding a youngster is to modify or change the behaviour of that youngster. It figures, then, that the purpose of aggressive behaviour towards us is to modify our behaviour. Something is not to the horse's liking. What could it be? It could be any number of things, or a combination of several.

Look at the list of dislikes again. Is there anything that rings a bell, or makes you think – hmmm, that could be it? When and where does this apply to you? Whatever it is, or wherever it is, this is the area you need to work on.

Here are some suggestions:

Are you nervous in any way?
You need to act 'as if' you are confident and know what you are doing.

Are you making assumptions about what he can or can't, should or should not do?
Observe and listen to the horse. He will tell you what he can or can't do.

Are you taking the horse for granted?
Make friends with him and find out whether or not he has been trained to do the things you expected of him.

Are you approaching him with too much enthusiasm or determination?
Slow down.

Are you too brisk and efficient?
Again, slow down and soften in your manner.

Are you too affectionate?
Treat him like a horse, not a cuddly child.

Do you get the idea? Something in your manner is annoying him. When his behaviour is really vicious, I regret to say that your very presence is annoying him intensely.

That said, there are a few horses (not many, thankfully) who have been so badly abused that they have a hatred of all people. I have only ever seen two such horses in my life. One was a stallion, used for breeding purposes. He only ever came out of his stable to cover a mare. His bedding, if that's what it can be called, was knee-deep in muck. Evidently, straw was only thrown in every now and then; nothing was ever taken out. The door to his stable had thick, strong mesh above it. As we approached the door, he came at the mesh, baring his teeth and snarling like a caged tiger. This horse did not like people.

The second one I saw was actually at a veterinary hospital. This horse had a large, airy pen, with a high gate in front of it. As I passed the pen (without going anywhere near it) the horse went berserk. He charged round the pen like a lunatic, flattening his ears, kicking wildly and baring his teeth as he approached the gate. This horse didn't like people either. The mere sight of one was enough to drive him nuts.

WHAT I WOULD I DO FOR THESE HORSES

I would let the stallion out of his cage and turn him out in a nice pasture – preferably with a few mares. Any mares I wanted him to cover would be turned out with him. In any case, conception is more likely when mating takes place naturally. He would be treated like a normal horse, caught and handled only when necessary. Otherwise, he would be left alone to live the life of a normal, natural horse. Of course, if I started with him as he was, I would have a devil of a job to catch him. My first task would therefore be to make friends with him and show him that he could trust me. It would take a long time but, eventually, he would allow himself to be caught, like any normal horse. I would also never put him back in a stable, unless absolutely necessary. He would probably have a fear of stables like no other.

For the other horse, I would start by gaining his trust and friendship in a pen. If he were loose in a field, it would take forever for him to stop running a mile at the mere sight of me. I would spend a lot of time just being there, at first outside the pen and later, as his trust increased, in the pen with him.

I wouldn't say much and I would do nothing. I would just 'hang about' and wait for him to come to me. I would also have a pocketful of treats at the ready, so when he came to me, he would be well rewarded.

When I had won his complete trust and confidence in the pen, I would turn him out in a small field or paddock, with a headcollar on. I would put him on his own, to capitalise on his innate need for company and make my presence that bit more desirable. There, I would adopt much the same procedure, hanging about, waiting for him to come to me. Then he would get much praise and more treats. When that was as it should be, I would start playing around with catching him, taking hold of his headcollar and seeing how he responded to that.

When that was OK, I would clip a lead-rope on, to find out how he felt about being led. In all probability, he would be OK, but at this point it's purely hypothetical. It would depend on what happened at each subsequent stage of the game – but you doubtless get the idea. I would treat him like a wild horse who had never been touched or handled by people.

RESPONDING TO AGGRESSION

What to do with your aggressive horse is any variation on this theme. You must find out what's bothering him and put it right. As often as not, it means taking a long, hard look at yourself. You have to know what he dislikes, either about you, or the way you are doing things.

Interpreting the signs

Aggressive behaviour almost always starts with warning signs, which we ignore at our peril: a lifted hind leg, flattened ears, a swing of the head towards us. The horse looks ugly and his intentions are clear. The first rule of thumb is to SHOW NO FEAR. As soon as we do anything submissive, like move rapidly out of the way, we put him in a position of dominance. Whatever else we do, this must not be allowed to happen. Better by far is to 'bite back' with a loud, angry shout: 'How dare you do that!' This, however, is just the instantaneous reaction. We must also get to the bottom of his aggressive behaviour and understand why he is doing it.

Issues with handling

As mentioned earlier, most commonly aggression comes from a strong dislike of things we do or ask the horse to do. For example, we may be pulling the girth up too far and fast for his liking. He feels the breath squeezed out of him and it makes him angry. He swings his head to warn us, or he may nip. If we ignore the warning and carry on as we are, nipping will soon turn to biting. So we think about what we are doing and fasten the girth more slowly and gently. 'Thank you', says the horse. 'That's just what I wanted!'

General handling and grooming can also lead to aggressive behaviour. Rugging is often a particular problem. This is an interesting one. It is my contention that most horses don't need rugs. They all grow the coat they need. Nipping or biting while putting on a rug seems to bear out my theory. It is my belief that horses who object strongly to their rugs know they don't need them and this is what they are trying to say. The answer, then, couldn't be easier. Stop using a rug!

When I was growing up, horses lived out without a rug as a matter of course. It was considered perfectly normal. Noticeably, they never took any harm from it. I even knew of racehorses, wintering out on the Essex marshes, without a rug between them. Slowly, rugs have become 'a convenience' and are now considered a necessity. The horse who objects by nipping or biting may be telling us otherwise. As far as the horse is concerned, rugs are anything but essential.

What's coming next?

This is the 'We've been here before' response: there is something about his ridden time that the horse dislikes intensely. Knowing what is coming, he starts voicing his objections during preparation, grooming, tacking-up, etc. He may even start soon after being caught – if he has allowed himself to be caught, that is. The message is the same. 'Leave me alone. Get out of space. I don't want you near me.'

If this is the case, you must assess your riding and make some changes. Are you making it uncomfortable? Do you get into frequent or regular fights? Is he bored by constant repetition in a small, enclosed space? Are you asking or expecting too much?

Reactions

In addition to trying to work out and remedy whatever is causing the aggressive behaviour, you may also need to respond to the behaviour itself. At the same time (strangely, perhaps) you must be relatively kind to the horse. That is to say, if you want to avoid a downward spiral of action and reaction, you must work towards moderating your response. Thus, the first time he bites or kicks, it's fine to shout or yell at him. A slap across the muzzle or on the rump is also permissible. And, sometimes, this works – but you can only ever do this once, or at the most, twice. After that, you downgrade to the language he understands perfectly and make your own threat gesture by raising your hand, *threatening* to strike and growling. If this doesn't make the point, you have to take a different approach. What you must not do is get stuck in a rut of mutual aggression.

The different approach is to carry on as best you can and talk to him kindly: 'Come on, old chap, there's no need for all this'. You can also give him a few fairly strong pats or slaps of affection, meanwhile watching his body language. If he looks threatening, this may not be appropriate. And, in case he tries to do so, be sure that he cannot make contact with his teeth or heels. Ignoring his scowls and showing appreciation where you can is usually the best way to go.

Bribery can also be quite effective. Instead of dodging his teeth or heels, feed him a few treats. If necessary, and if one is available, ask a handy helper to feed him treats while you get on with the job. Some horses just need us to be extra friendly, but we must go about this in the right way.

Treats, for example, can be a mixed blessing. A frequent cause of biting is over-indulgence. This comes from an owner who randomly and constantly hands out treats. This serves no useful purpose at all, but makes the horse greedy and constantly wanting more. When he doesn't get any more, he gets really annoyed and bites the hand that doesn't feed him. This message is very clear. It says, 'You're mean. I don't like you.'

This horse has to learn that treats are no longer forthcoming. They must be withdrawn immediately. Any subsequent aggressive behaviour must be dealt with sharply. At the same time, you must be kind to him in every way possible. This doesn't mean soft. It means kind consideration, but with a firm hand. You must also show your appreciation with lots of words of praise and kindly pats on the neck whenever there is progress.

Avoiding extremes

Nervous handling

As mentioned previously, one source of angst is nervous handling – being too soft and fiddling about too much. The horse picks up on this and says: 'Stay away from me then. I don't do nervous handling.' The answer here is to play the 'let's pretend' game and act as if you know what you are doing and are full of confidence. Generally, you *do* know what to do – it's just that the delivery that isn't right. If necessary, make the process short and sweet. Without actually hurrying or being careless, get it over and done with – and don't fiddle about!

Too much confidence

Conversely, handling that is too brisk can be objectionable to a sensitive horse. Although he can only react with 'Leave me alone' (his vocabulary is limited) he will accept slower, softer handling as a suitable compromise.

Horses show affection by standing close to each other and, sometimes, by mutual grooming.

Too much petting

Some horses really dislike too much petting, fussing etc. They feel smothered by it. Between themselves, they only show affection (if that's what it is) by standing and/or grazing close to each other. Any physical contact is confined to mutual grooming. Thus, the best way to show affection and/or appreciation is with the odd bit of patting or friendly slapping. Nothing more!

You may also find that there are areas where horses really like a bit of scratching. Under the mane or forelock are often good places. Some also like a good hard rub or scratch on the rump around the tail area. They tell you when they've had enough, simply by moving away.

THE INCURABLES

Finally, there are some, usually performance horses of one type or another, who kick up a fuss in the stable. No matter how good or appropriate the handling, the habit doesn't go away. My personal theory is that they don't like being performance horses. The work goes against their natural horsy instincts and is too hard for their liking, but being as well trained as they are, they do the job to the best of their ability. Besides, the work they have to do demands a lot of energy, so any adrenalin build-up from the anger they feel is dissipated during work.

Anyone who has such a horse can only make the best of a bad job. Cross-tying (i.e. a tie-rope from either side of the headcollar) helps to keep the teeth out of range and can sometimes also keep the horse calm, because he knows he is beaten – not literally of course, but horses are good at submitting when they have no choice.

SUMMARY

❖ Aggressive behaviour is intended to make us modify or change our behaviour.

❖ It is for us to work out what the horse is trying to tell us.

❖ Find the answer in his likes and dislikes.

❖ Watch out for warning signs, i.e. threat gestures.

❖ Show no fear.

❖ A short, sharp retaliation is permissible, but not more than twice.

❖ Take a long, hard look at what you are doing/the way you are doing it.

❖ Too much confidence can be as annoying as nervous handling.

❖ Consider other areas he may dislike or find difficult, such as riding.

❖ Gain his trust, make friends with him, but treat him like a horse, not a fluffy pet.

❖ Bribery can be effective in moderation.

❖ Give praise and show appreciation for every good thing he does.

❖ Accepting him the way he is and cross-tying may be the only solution.

CONCLUSION

When handling horses, I often think of what I call 'the old boy grooms'. In days gone by, they were employed by the rich to look after their horses. They did everything for the horses except ride them. They were patience personified. Everything about them was slow, careful, considerate and, perhaps above all – dignified. They knew horses inside out. Without a doubt, they had the love and respect of every horse in their care. They knew the individual needs and personalities of every single one.

Unfortunately, the old boy grooms are long gone, but we can still learn from them. We can bring the image to mind of a rather elderly man (OK, they were young once!) whistling softly through his teeth as he methodically gets on with what he has to do. He never rushes or hassles a horse. His hands are strong, firm and reassuring, and he knows exactly when and how to use them. He talks to them in a soft, slow, kindly voice: 'Come on, old girl. Move yourself over. There we are. That feels good, doesn't it?' … that kind of thing.

I think if there is one word that sums up the manner in which we should approach and handle the horse, it is 'dignified'. If we treat the horse with dignity, we get respect and cooperation back. If we are lucky, we even get his version of affection; the friendly nuzzle, the welcome whinny, but best of all, we get an honest, friendly horse.

* * * * *

I hope you have found this book interesting, informative and above all, useful. I am saddened by the continuing rise of problem behaviour in horses. There is no need for it – but that's another story! Unfortunately, when problems do arise, whatever the cause, we have to deal with them, but we owe it to the horse to do the right thing and put his world to rights. I hope to have conveyed to you that it isn't so difficult, as long as we know what to do and how to do it. A little understanding goes a long way.

INDEX